PSALM 91

PEGGY JOYCE RUTH

Psalm 91
Peggy Joyce Ruth

Copyright © 2002
Peggy Joyce Ruth BETTER LIVING Ministries
www.peggyjoyceruth.org
All rights reserved.

Printed in the United States of America by Codra

ISBN 978-0-89228-178-7
Library of Congress Control Number: 2002110752

Ninth Printing, 2015

Cover by Marcus Stallworth
Edit by Roberta Wescott

Contents

Psalm 91 Testimonies

Foreword

In the midst of these turbulent times, God has anointed Peggy Joyce to write this wonderful book, *Psalm 91: God's Umbrella of Protection.*

When someone has walked in a Truth of God for over 40 years, there is a depth of insight incomparable to anything else. Such is the case of Peggy Ruth, our dear friend and partner in the ministry. What a gift she is to the Body of Christ! She is a pastor's wife, Bible teacher, radio host and author. And there is no fluff to Peggy! She is Rock solid and has earned the right to be listened to. From her personal furnace of affliction, she has effectively explained this famous psalm and challenged us to new levels of faith and trust in God.

This is more than an inspiring book. It is a parent's manual, a leader's handbook, a pastor's promise and a Christian's covenant. I wholeheartedly recommend this book. It contains both inspiration and information which remains Biblically sound.

Along with this much needed book, Tommy and I applaud both Jack and Peggy Joyce for their unwavering faithfulness to their many assignments from the Lord. Their lives are a book!

Rachel Burchfield
President of Texas Bible Institute

Foreword

I have always loved the 91st Psalm, and I've known it to be the chapter of God's promises of protection for believers. It has been very helpful to read the books that Peggy Joyce Ruth has written on Psalm 91, because Holy Spirit has helped her dissect it and get the meat out to feed those of us who are hungry to know everything that will nourish us, give us strength, and allow us to grow and mature into the sons and daughters of The Most High God.

I have hidden the Word in my heart and found that in my times of need, Holy Spirit brings it to my remembrance. When I receive it, and speak it, it brings results. In the beginning was the Word, and the Word was with God, and the Word was God! That settles it! We need to know the Promises of God in His Word to apply to our lives until our faith grows to the stature and measure of Jesus Christ.

THANK YOU Peggy Joyce Ruth for digging into the Word of Psalm 91 to help us digest the strength made available to those who have ears to hear. God bless you, and all who hunger and thirst for TRUTH! It will set you FREE!

Love in Him who Loved us first...

Mama Shirley Boone
WE WIN MINISTRIES
Ryan's Reach.com
The Boone Center For The Family at Pepperdine University
Mercy Corps International Humanitarian Organization

Introduction

Are you tired of tormenting fear thoughts that seem to always be lurking just below the surface, ready to control your life and steal your peace and well-being? If so, I think you will find the message in this book is the answer you've been searching for.

Maybe you fear the dangers that face your children everyday—peer pressure, drugs or alcohol. I, too, faced those fears. I also used I battled the nagging anxiety over what I would do if my husband, Jack, was in a car wreck, had a sudden heart attack or was involved in some other tragedy that might claim his life.

Those fears that tormented my imagination used to be my constant companions. Yet, it was easy to justify them with all that was going on in the world!

Back in the 1950s things were fairly predictable, but the word *predictable* was becoming more obsolete with each passing decade. Fear was running rampant because of the uncertainty of the times—cancer, natural disasters, financial difficulties and terrorism were everywhere I turned. But after all, didn't the Bible tell us in Matthew 24, "*In the last days men's hearts will fail because of fear?"* Somehow it consoled me to know I was not alone in my dilemma.

But one Sunday changed everything. That's the day the Lord miraculously, through a dream, spoke to me from a psalm I had never heard of before and answered my question—*"Is there any way to be protected from all the things that are coming on the earth?"* When I awoke, peace—like warm oil—flowed over me.

From that supernatural Word from God and the months of research that followed, I came to realize Psalm 91 was not merely something to bring comfort to me during times of sorrow. I saw it was there to take me *victoriously* through *any* crisis I might encounter.

This book is the result of the longing in my heart to help people who are struggling with the same fears I agonized over for so long. If this is something you already know, then God wants to remind you of this truth.

I encourage you to mark these scriptures in your own Bible as we go straight through this psalm. This is God's *covenant of protection* for you personally.

My prayer is that Psalm 91 will give you the **courage to trust!**

Setting the Scene

Sundays were usually a comfort. For some reason being inside the church building made the fears temporarily disappear—but not on this particular Sunday!

Our pastor looked unusually serious that day as he made the announcement that one of our most beloved and faithful deacons had been diagnosed with leukemia and had only a few weeks to live. Only the Sunday before this robust-looking deacon in his mid-forties had been in his regular place in the choir — looking as healthy and happy as ever. Now, one Sunday later, the entire congregation was in a state of shock after hearing such an unexpected announcement.

Several of the members got upset with the pastor when he said, "*Get out all of your silly little get-well cards and start sending them.*" But I completely understood the frustration that had initiated the remark. However, little did I know this incident would pave the way to a ***MESSAGE THAT WAS GOING TO FOREVER BURN IN MY HEART.***

Surprisingly, I had gone home from church that day feeling very little fear, perhaps because I was numb from the shock of what I had heard. I vividly remember sitting down on the edge of the bed that afternoon and saying out loud, "*Lord, is there any way to be protected from all the evils that are coming on the earth?*"

I was not expecting an answer. I was merely voicing the thought that kept going over and over in my mind. I remember lying across the bed and falling immediately to sleep, only to wake up a short five minutes later. However, in those five minutes I had a very unusual dream.

In the dream I was in an open field, asking the same question I had prayed earlier — "*Is there any way to be protected from all the things that are coming on the earth?*" And in my dream I heard these words:

"In your day of trouble call upon Me, and I will answer you!"

Suddenly, I knew I had the answer I had so long been searching for. The ecstatic joy I felt was beyond anything I could ever describe. And instantly, to my surprise, there were hundreds of Christians with me in the dream out in that open field, praising and thanking God for the answer. But it wasn't until the next day when I heard the 91st Psalm referred to on a tape by Shirley Boone that suddenly—I *knew in my heart* that **whatever** was in that psalm was God's answer to my question. I nearly tore up my Bible in my haste to see what it said. And there it was in verse 15—the *exact statement* God had spoken to me in my dream. I could hardly believe my eyes!

I believe that you who are reading this book are among the many Christians who were pictured with me in that open field, who will, through the Message in this book, get your answer to the question, "Can a Christian be protected through these turbulent times?"

Since the early 1970s, I have had many opportunities to share this message. I believe God has commissioned me to write this book to proclaim God's *Covenant of Protection*. May you be sincerely blessed by it.

Peggy Joyce Ruth

Psalm 91

He who dwells in the shelter of the Most High
Will abide in the shadow of the Almighty.
I will say to the Lord, "My refuge and my fortress,
My God, in whom I trust!"
For it is He who delivers you from the snare of the trapper
And from the deadly pestilence.
He will cover you with His pinions,
And under His wings you may seek refuge;
His faithfulness is a shield and bulwark.

You will not be afraid of the terror by night,
Or of the arrow that flies by day;
Of the pestilence that stalks in darkness,
Or of the destruction that lays waste at noon.
A thousand may fall at your side,
And ten thousand at your right hand;
But it shall not approach you.
You will only look on with your eyes,
And see the recompense of the wicked.
For you have made the Lord, my refuge,
Even the Most High, your dwelling place.

No evil will befall you,
Nor will any plague come near your tent.
For He will give His angels charge concerning you,
To guard you in all your ways.
They will bear you up in their hands,
Lest you strike your foot against a stone.
You will tread upon the lion and cobra,
The young lion and the serpent you will trample down.

Because he has loved Me, therefore I will deliver him;
I will set him securely on high,
Because he has known My name.
He will call upon Me, and I will answer him;
I will be with him in trouble;
I will rescue him, and honor him.
With a long life I will satisfy him,
And let him behold My salvation.

Chapter 1

Where Is My Dwelling Place?

He who dwells in the shelter of the Most High will abide in the shadow of the Almighty.   –Psalm 91:1

HAVE YOU EVER BEEN inside a cabin with a big roaring fire in the fireplace, enjoying this wonderful feeling of safety and security as you watched an enormous electrical storm going on outside? It was a warm, wonderful sensation, knowing you were being sheltered and protected from the storm. **That is what Psalm 91 is all about—shelter!**

Did you know there is a place in God—a secret place—for those who want to seek refuge? **It is a literal place of physical safety and security that God is referring to.**

Dwelling in the shelter of the Most High is the Old Testament's way of teaching faith. This gives us the most intense illustration of the very essence of personal relationship. Man has no innate built-in shelter. Alone, he stands shelterless against the elements and must run to THE SHELTER, which is God Himself. In verse one, God is offering us more than protection; it is as if He rolls out the hospitality mat and personally invites us in.

I am sure every one of you can think of something that represents *security* to you. When I think of security, shelter and protection, I have a childhood memory that automatically comes to mind. My parents would take me and my younger brother and sister out to a lake to fish for an afternoon of fun.

Dad had a secluded place on this lake near Brownwood where he would take us to fish for perch. That was the second greatest highlight of the outing. I loved seeing the cork begin to bobble, and then, suddenly, it would go completely out of sight. There were only a few things that could thrill me more than jerking back on that old cane pole and landing a huge perch right in the boat. I think I was grown before I realized Dad had an ulterior motive in taking us for an afternoon of perch fishing. Those perch were his bait for the trotline he had stretched out across one of the secret coves at the lake.

Dad would drive the boat over to the place where his trotline was located, then he would cut off the boat motor and inch the boat across the cove as he "*ran the trot line*." That's what he called it when he would hold onto the trotline with his hands and pull the boat alongside all the strategically placed, baited hooks to see if any of them had caught a large catfish.

I said that catching the perch was the *second* greatest highlight of the outing. By far, the greatest thrill was the times when Dad would get to a place where the trotline rope would begin to jerk almost out of his hand. It was then that we three siblings would watch—wide eyed—as Dad would wrestle with the line until finally, in victory, he would flip that huge catfish over the side of the boat, right on the floor board at our feet. Money couldn't buy that kind of excitement! The circus and carnival, all rolled up into one, couldn't compete with that kind of a thrill.

One of these outings proved more eventful than most—turning out to be an experience I will never forget. It had been a beautiful day when we started out, but by the time we had finished our perch fishing and were headed toward the cove, everything changed. A storm came up on the lake so suddenly that there was no time to get back to the boat dock. The sky turned black, lightning flashed, and drops of rain fell with such force they actually stung when they hit. Then, moments later we began to be pelted by large, marble-sized hailstones.

I saw the fear in my mother's eyes, and I knew we were in danger. But, before I had time to wonder what we were going to do, Dad had driven the boat to the rugged shoreline of the only island on the lake. Boat docks surround that island now, but back then it just looked like an abandoned island with absolutely no place to take cover.

Within moments Dad had us all out of the boat and ordered the three of us to lie down beside our mother on the ground. He quickly pulled a canvas tarp out of the bottom of the boat, knelt down on the ground beside us and thrust the tarp up over all five of us. That storm raged outside the makeshift tent he had fashioned over us; the rain beat down, the lightning flashed and the thunder rolled, yet I could think of nothing else but how it felt to have my dad's arms around us. There was a certain calm under the protection of the shield my father provided that is hard to explain now.

In fact, I had never felt as safe and secure in my entire life. I can remember thinking I wished the storm would last forever. I didn't want anything to spoil the wonderful security I felt that day *in our secret hiding place.* Feeling my father's protective arms around me, I never wanted the moment to end.

Although, I have never forgotten that experience, today it has taken on new meaning. Just as Dad had put a tarp over us that day to shield us from the storm, our Heavenly Father has a *Secret Place* in His arms that protects us from the storms raging in the world around us.

That *Secret Place* is literal, but it is also conditional! In verse one of Psalm 91, God lists our part of the condition before He even mentions the promises included in His part. That's because *our part* has to come first. In order to abide in the *shadow* of the Almighty, we must *choose to dwell* in the shelter of the Most High.

The question is—"*How do we dwell in the security and shelter of the Most High?*" It is more than an intellectual experience. It is a dwelling place where we can be physically protected if we run to Him. You may utterly believe that God is your refuge, you may give mental assent to it in your prayer time, you may teach Sunday school lessons on this concept of refuge, and you may even get a warm feeling every time you think of it, but unless you do something about it—*unless you actually get up and run to the shelter*—you will never experience it.

Corrie Ten Boom tells a story of a man who certainly acted on the protection of the Most High! An Englishman, in WWII, who was held in a German prison camp for a long period of time, came to know the Lord. One day he read Psalm 91. "Father in heaven," he prayed, "I see all these men dying around me, one after the other. Will I also have to die here? I am still young and I very much want to work in Your kingdom here on earth."

He received this answer: "Rely on what you have just read and go home!" Trusting in the Lord, he got up and walked into the corridor toward the gate. A guard called out, "Prisoner, where are you going?"

"I am under the protection of the Most High," he replied. The guard came to attention and let him pass, for Adolf Hitler was known as "the Most High." He came to the gate, where a group of guards stood. They commanded him to stop and asked where he was going. "I am under the protection of the Most High." All the guards stood at attention as he walked out the gate.

The English officer made his way through the German countryside and eventually reached England, where he told how he had made his escape. He was the **only one** to come out of that prison alive. [1]

You also might call that place of refuge—a *Love Walk*! In fact, the secret place is, in reality, the intimacy and familiarity of the presence of God Himself. When our grandchildren, Cullen and Meritt, ages ten and seven, stay the night with us, the moment they finish breakfast, each runs to his own secret place to spend some time talking with God. Cullen finds a place behind the couch in the family room, and Meritt heads behind the lamp table in the corner of our bedroom. Those places have become very special to them.

Where is your secret place? You, too, need the security and shelter of a secret place with the Most High. This place of refuge is actually a relationship with the Father you have cultivated and developed by investing enough time into it to make it very personal and intimate.

---

[1] *Corrie Ten Boom's book: **Clippings from My Notebook** pages 41–42*

Chapter 2

What is Coming Out of My Mouth?

I will say to the Lord, "My Refuge and my Fortress, my God, in whom I trust!" —Psalm 91:2

NOTICE VERSE TWO SAYS, "*I will say...*" Circle the word "*say*" in your Bible because we must learn to verbalize our trust. We answer back to God what He said to us in the first verse. There is power in saying His Word back to Him!

We are not told to just *think* the Word. We are told to *say* the Word. For example, Joel 3:10 tells the weak to say, "*I am a mighty man.*" Over and over we find great men of God such as David, Joshua, Shadrach, Meshach and Abednego declaring their confessions of faith out loud in dangerous situations. Notice what begins to happen on the inside when you say, "*Lord, You are my Refuge — You are my Fortress — You are my Lord and my God! It is in You that I put my total trust!*" The more we say it out loud, the more confident we become in His protection.

So many times, as Christians, we mentally agree that the Lord is our Refuge — but that is not good enough. *Power is released* in saying it out loud. When we say it, and mean it, we are placing ourselves in His shelter. By *voicing* His Lordship and His Protection we *walk in the door* to the secret place.

One cannot miss the fact that this verse uses the word *my* three times: "my refuge...my fortress...my God!" The psalmist makes a personal claim to God. The reason we can trust is that we know who God is to us. This verse makes the analogy of who God is; He is a refuge and a fortress. God Himself becomes the defensive site for us against all invading enemies. He is personally our protection.

Some quote Psalm 91 as though it were some *magical wand*, but there is nothing magical about this psalm. It is powerful and it works simply because it is the Word of God—alive and active. And, we confess it out loud, simply because the Bible tells us to.

There is, however, a uniqueness about this psalm. Promises of protection can be found throughout the Bible; but Psalm 91 is the only place in the Word where all of the protection promises are brought together in one collection—forming a covenant written through the Holy Spirit. How powerful that is!

Have you ever tried to protect yourself from all the bad things that can happen? It's like trying to keep the whole law. God knows we can't do it. Psalms 60:11b tells us *"...deliverance by man is in vain."* God has to be our Source before the promises in Psalm 91 will ever work.

We could go to the doctor once a month for a checkup. We could double check our cars every day to see that the motor, the tires and the brakes were all in good running order. We could fireproof our houses and store up food for a time of need. Yet, we still couldn't do enough to protect ourselves from every potential danger. It's impossible!

It isn't that any one of these precautions is wrong. It is that not one of these things, in and of itself, has the power to protect. God has to be the One to whom we run first. **He is the only One who has an answer for *whatever* might come.**

> *"For I know the plans that I have for you," declares the Lord, "plans for welfare and not for calamity to give you a future and a hope."*
> —Jeremiah 29:11

When I think of how utterly impossible it is to protect ourselves from all the evils that are in the world, I always think of a sheep. A sheep has no real protection other than its shepherd. In fact, it is the only animal I can think of that has *no* built-in protection. It has no sharp teeth, no offensive odor to spray to drive off its enemies, no loud bark, and it certainly can't run fast enough to escape danger. That's why the Bible calls us God's sheep! God is saying, "*I want you to see Me as your Source of protection. I am your Shepherd.*" Now, He may use doctors, storm cellars or bank accounts to meet our specific needs, but our hearts have to run to Him first as our Shepherd and our Protector. Then, *He* will choose the method He desires to bring about the protection.

When I'm facing a challenge I have learned to say out loud, *"In this particular situation*_____ (name the situation out loud) *I choose to trust you, Lord."* The difference it makes when I proclaim my trust out loud is amazing.

Take notice of what flies out of your mouth in times of trouble. The worst thing that can happen is for something to come out that brings death. Cursing gives God nothing to work with. This psalm tells us to do just the opposite—speak life! One of those times that brought life to a death situation really stands out in my mind: The whole family was rejoicing when our daughter-in-law, Sloan, received a positive pregnancy test report and found that she was going to have the first grandchild on either side of the family. Since she'd had a tubal pregnancy once before that resulted in a miscarriage, making her highly susceptible for another, the doctor then ordered a sonogram as a precautionary measure.

The disturbing result of the sonogram was—*"no fetus found, a great deal of water in the uterus and spots of endometriosis."* With only two hour's notice, emergency surgery was quickly underway, at which time the doctor performed a laparoscopy, drained the uterus, and scraped away the endometriosis. After the surgery the doctor's words were, *"During the laparoscopy we carefully looked everywhere, and there was no sign of a baby, but I want to see you back in my office in one week to be sure fluid doesn't build back up."* When Sloan argued that the pregnancy test had been positive, he said there was a 99 percent chance the baby had naturally aborted and had been absorbed back into the uterine lining.

After he left the room Sloan was the only one not fazed by the doctor's report. What she said next surprised everyone. She emphatically stated that even the doctor had left her with a one percent chance, and she was going to take it. From that moment, no amount of discouragement from well-meaning friends who didn't want her to be disappointed had any effect on her. Never once did she veer from confessing out loud Psalm 91 and another Scripture promise that she had found: —*"My child will live, and not die, and declare the wonderful works of God (Psalm 118:17)."* A treasured book that was very important to Sloan during this time was *Supernatural Childbirth* by Jackie Mize.

A strange look came on the technician's face the next week as she administered the ultrasound. She immediately called for the physician. Her reaction was a little disconcerting to Sloan until she heard the words—*"Doctor, I think you need to come here quickly. I've just found a six week old fetus!"* It was nothing short of a miracle that such severe, invasive procedures had not damaged or destroyed this delicate beginning stage of life. When I look at my grandson, it is hard to imagine life without him. I thank God for a daughter-in-law who believes in her covenant and is not ashamed *to confess it out loud* in the face of every negative report.

Our part of this protection covenant is expressed in verses one and two—"he who *dwells...*" and "he who *says...*" This releases His power to bring about the promises in verses three through sixteen.

Chapter 3

Two-Way Deliverance

For it is He who delivers you from the snare of the trapper and from the deadly pestilence. —Psalm 91:3

HAVE YOU EVER SEEN a movie where a fur trapper travels deep into the mountains in the cold climate? He baits big, steel traps, covers them over with branches and then waits for some unsuspecting animal to step into the trap. Those traps were not there by chance. The trapper had taken great care in placing them in very strategic locations.

That is a picture of what the enemy does to us. That's why he is called the *trapper!* The traps set for us are not there by accident. It is as if your name is on it. They are custom made, placed and baited specifically for each one of us. But like an animal caught in a trap, it is a slow, painful process. You don't die instantly. You are ensnared until the trapper comes to destroy you.

The enemy knows exactly what will most likely hook us, and he knows exactly which *thought* to put into our minds to lure us into the trap. That is why Paul tells us in 2 Corinthians 2:11 that we are *"...not to be ignorant of the schemes (traps) of the enemy."* Then he says:

> *For the weapons of our warfare are not of the flesh but divinely powerful for the destruction of fortresses. We are destroying speculations and every lofty thing raised up against the knowledge of God, and we are taking every thought captive to the obedience of Jesus Christ.* —2 Corinthians 10:4-5

God not only delivers us from the snare laid by the trapper (Satan), but according to the last part of verse three, He also delivers us from the deadly *pestilence.* I always thought a pestilence was something that attacked crops — bugs, locusts, grasshoppers, spider mites, mildew and root rot. After doing a word study on the word *pestilence,* however, I found, to my surprise, that pestilence attacks people — not crops! A pestilence is any lethal disease.

Webster's New World Dictionary says pestilence is *"any virulent or fatal disease; an epidemic that hits the masses of people—any deadly disease that attaches itself to one's body with the intent to destroy."* But, God says, *"I will deliver you from the deadly disease that comes with the intent to destroy."*

There are all kinds of enemies: temptations, spiritual enemies, and physical enemies. Initially, I was in a quandary wondering if God really meant *literal* pestilence. It took me awhile to see the internal workings of warfare in the body as a parallel concept with disease. Only man tries to choose between physical and spiritual deliverance; the Scripture encases both. (Notice how Jesus demonstrates that His power operates at all levels with a very literal, physical fulfillment in Matthew 8:16-17). When evil is served it looks the same on the platter. Scripture deals with both through clear verses that promise physical healing and literal deliverance.

God is so good to confirm His Word when one seeks Him with an open heart. Right after I had received the dream about Psalm 91 and was trying to digest all of these protection promises and comprehend the fact that God is the One who always sends good and not evil, Satan was on the other end trying to discourage my faith at every turn. Because I was very young in my conviction and struggling hard to maintain it in the midst of a world that does not believe in the supernatural *goodness* of God, I was devastated when a thought came into my mind one morning as I was getting ready to go to church. *"If God wants us to walk in health, why did He create germs?"* That one thought was attempting to completely dismantle my faith in this *new-found truth* that God had provided healing in the atonement. In fact, I was so distraught that I didn't even think I could motivate myself to go to church that morning.

I remember I went into my bedroom and literally fell on my face before God, asking Him how those two facts could possibly be reconciled. As clear as a bell, God spoke in my spirit, *"Trust Me, get up and go, and I will give you an answer."* I got up with mixed emotions. I had unmistakably heard God speak to my spirit, but I could see no way in which He could satisfactorily resolve the question that had struck in my head. *Why **would** God create a germ to make us sick, if He did, in fact, want us to walk in divine health?*

I went to church that morning under a cloud of heaviness, and I couldn't tell you what subject the pastor preached on. But, somewhere in the middle of his sermon he made a random statement, "God made everything good. Take germs, for instance—germs are nothing more than microscopic plants and animals that *the enemy* perverted and uses to spread disease." Then, he just stopped and with a very strange look on his face said, "I have no idea where that thought came from. It was not in my notes," and went right on with his sermon. I must admit I almost disturbed the entire service because I couldn't keep from bouncing up and down on the pew. The awesomeness of God was more than I could take in without it erupting out of me. God could not have done anything that would have strengthened my faith for healing more than that incident did that morning.

Do you sometimes feel you have opposition facing you from every side? This verse is addressing the enemy's assignments from both the physical, as well as the spiritual. One of our family members went to a certain country as a missionary and made the comment, "This is a country where there are numerous ways to die." Both the poor health conditions and the hostility in the country provided many dangers. There are enemies that attack your mind (thoughts), some that attack your body (germs) and some who attack you physically (people). This is your verse that insures your deliverance from all the varieties of harm.

Consider with me one more area of physical protection from harm. When Jesus sent the disciples out, He gave these instructions, *"I send you out as sheep among wolves. Be as wise as serpents, but be harmless as doves (Matthew 10:16)."* It is an interesting piece of information to be told to have the cleverness of a snake (in order not to be harmed), but also the innocence of a dove (in order not to cause harm).

Each year at the Texas Rattlesnake Roundup, men often disassemble rattlesnakes with their knives for the gaping audience. Before milking the snake of its poison, they slice open the thick, scaly skin covering with its agile muscular structure and pry open the snake's mouth to reveal the fangs. After seeing the internal workings, it becomes obvious that the snake is geared for causing harm. Not so with the dove. When a hunter cleans a dove, first he pulls off the feathers. There are no thick scales, no dangerous claws, no poisonous venom... The dove has nothing in him that causes harm. In this analogy we are advised as sheep among wolves to be as clever as the snake, but as innocent as the dove. This takes care of harm in two directions. I believe you can claim the promise of this verse—for God to protect you from being harmed and from your harming innocent people. Defensively pray, for example, that God protects you from ever hitting a child on a bicycle, being involved in a wreck that kills another person, causing someone to walk away from the faith… Many a person has been traumatized from inadvertently hurting someone he never intended to hurt. God has this preventative promise in verse three for us to stand on for protection from both ways in which harm can destroy a life.

In the same way, notice the two-fold aspect to this deliverance in verse three: from the **snare of the trapper** and from the **deadly pestilence.** This covers being delivered from *temptation* and being delivered from *harm.* It is similar to the request in the Lord's Prayer. *"Lead us away from temptation and deliver us from evil."* What good would it do to be delivered from harm—only to be caught in a sin that destroys us? On the other hand, what good would it do to be delivered from a sin—only to be destroyed by a deadly pestilence? This verse covers both. Thank God for His deliverance from both *traps* and *pestilence.*

Chapter 4

Under His Wings

He will cover you with His pinions, and under His wings,
you may seek refuge.   —Psalm 91:4a

W HEN YOU PICTURE A magnificent flying bird, it is
usually not a chicken that comes to mind. I've never
seen a chicken pictured in flight—many eagles, but no chickens.
We quote the Scripture from Isaiah 40:31 that talks about
being borne up on the wings of eagles or with wings like
eagles. There is a difference, however, between being "on"
His wings and being "under" His wings. This promise
in Psalm 91 is not elaborating on the *flying* wing—
but on the *sheltering* wing. One indicates strength and
accomplishment, while the other denotes protection and
familiarity. When you picture the warmth of a nest and the
security of being under the wings of the nurturing love of a
mother hen with chicks, it paints a vivid picture of the
sheltering wing of God's protection that the psalmist refers
to in this passage.

Is everyone protected under the wings? Did you notice it says He will cover you with His pinions (feathers), and under His wings, you *may* seek refuge? Again, it's up to us to make that decision! We can seek refuge under His wings, if we *choose* to.

The Lord gave me a vivid picture of what it means to seek refuge under His wings. My husband, Jack, and I live out in the country, and one spring our old mother hen hatched a brood of baby chickens. One afternoon when they were scattered all over the yard, I suddenly saw the shadow of a hawk overhead. I then noticed something very unique that taught me a lesson I will never forget. That mother hen did not run to those little chicks and jump on top of them to try to cover them with her wings. No!

Instead, she squatted down, spread out her wings and began to cluck. And those little chickens, from every direction, came running *to her* to get under those outstretched wings. Then, she pulled her wings down tight, tucking every little chick safely under her. To get to those babies, the hawk would have to have gone through the mother.

When I think of those baby chicks running to their mother, I realize it is under His (God's) wings where we *may* seek refuge—but we have to run to Him. *"He will cover you with His pinions, and under His wings, you may seek refuge."* That one little word **may** is a strong word! It is up to us! All that mother hen did was cluck and expand her wings to tell them where to come.

Oh, Jerusalem, Jerusalem... How often I wanted to gather your children together, the way a hen gathers her chicks under her wings, and you were unwilling.
                                                                    –Matthew 23:37

Notice the contrast between His willingness and our unwillingness—His *wanting to* against our *not willing to*— His *would* against our *would not*. What an amazing analogy to show us theologically that there is protection offered that we don't accept!

It is interesting that Jesus uses the correlation of *maternal* love to demonstrate His attachment to us. There is a certain fierceness to motherly-love we cannot overlook. God is deeply committed to us—yet, at the same time, we can reject His outstretched arms if we so choose. It is available, but not automatic. God does not run here and there, trying to cover us. He said, "*I have made protection possible. You run to Me!*" And, when we do run to Him in faith, **the enemy will have to go through God to get to us!** What a comforting thought!

Chapter 5

A Mighty Fortess Is My God

His faithfulness is a shield and bulwark.   –Psalm 91:4b

I T IS *GOD'S FAITHFULNESS* to His promises that is our shield. It is not just *our* faithfulness! God will be faithful to the promises He has made. When the enemy comes to whisper fearful or condemning thoughts in our mind, we can ward off his attack by saying, "*My faith is strong because I know My God is faithful, and His faithfulness is my shield!*"

How often I've heard people say, "*I can't dwell in the shelter of God. I mess up and fall short too many times. I feel guilty and unworthy.*" God knows all about our weaknesses. That's why He gave His Son. We can no more earn this protection, or deserve it, than we can earn or deserve our salvation. The main thing is—if we slip and fall, we must not stay down. Get up, repent and get back under that shield of protection. Thankfully this verse says it is His faithfulness, not ours, that is our shield.

If we are faithless, He remains faithful; for He cannot
deny Himself.   –2 Timothy 2:13

We must not point to what we've done, or haven't done.
We must point to what Jesus has done for us. **We dwell in
His shelter by faith in God's grace.** (Ephesians 2:8-9) And
faith is not hard.   It is simply our response to what Jesus has
already provided through His Blood. We cannot perform
enough good deeds to keep ourselves   in   His   shelter
anymore than we can do enough to keep ourselves saved. We
have to realize we dwell in His shelter, not in our own
righteousness, but in the Righteousness of Jesus Christ.

For by His doing, you are **in Christ Jesus who
became to us** *wisdom from God, and* **righteousness...**
                                    –1 Corinthians 1:30

There is a difference, however, between making an
occasional mistake and staying in willful sin. Self-will and
rebellion will keep us out of the secret place of protection
because self-will is a wall we build between God and us.

Our daughter slipped and fell face down in the busiest
4-way intersection in our city. Embarrassment made her
want to keep lying there so she didn't have to look up and
show her face to so many people who would know her in a
small town. Yet, the worst thing she could have done was

to lie there in that heavy traffic area. This is a humorous illustration of what it looks like when we fall spiritually. When you think of my daughter lying face down in the middle of the street, don't ever forget that the worst thing you can do after you fall spiritually is **fail to get up!**

Psalm 91:4b expresses again God's commitment and faithfulness to being our shield of protection. It is His faithfulness that gets us back on our feet and moving again. His unshakable faithfulness is a literal shield. I have this awesome mental picture of a huge shield in front of me, completely hiding me from the enemy. And, the shield is God Himself. His faithfulness to His promises guarantees us that His shield will remain forever steadfast and available, but whether or not we stay behind the protection of that shield is our choice.

Sometimes we have no power to rescue ourselves and we have to rely solely on His faithfulness. I saw this illustrated during one of the floods we had in our town several years ago. Our twenty year old son, Bill, had a flock of goats on some land by the bayou. As the bayou water began to rise and overflow its banks, some men saw Bill's goats being overtaken by the flood. They hoisted the goats up into the loft of a barn to keep them from drowning. By the next morning the water was like a rushing river—a mile wide—

washing away uprooted trees and everything else in its path. Bill had, by this time, been told about his goats, so, in spite of the road blocks and the rapids gushing by, he set out in an old tin bottom boat across those swift flood waters to rescue his little flock. He knew that in another few hours they would die from thirst and suffocation.

Little Willie was the most precious of all the herd because of the time Bill had spent bottle feeding him. The cry of that little goat was the first Bill heard when he got close to the barn. And, as you might expect, once Bill forced the loft door open amid the rushing waters, Little Willie was the first to jump into his arms. Then, boat load by boat load, goat by goat, Bill was able to get every one of those animals out of the loft and rowed to safety.

A television camera crew from Abilene, while filming the flood, caught sight of the little 'goat boy' risking his life to rescue his goats. That was the news story of the day, making the broadcast at six o'clock, and again at ten. It was a heartwarming story, but every time I think of Bill rescuing those goats that were in trouble, I think of how God sees us in our troubles and finds ways to rescue us.

Bill had to risk his own life to save Little Willie when the goat had no means of rescuing himself. This reminds me of the verse where Jesus talks about the times a shepherd must leave everything to go after the one sheep that needs help—which is, in fact, the Gospel in a nutshell. The shepherd lifts that sheep onto his shoulder and carries him back to safety. In the same way *God's faithfulness* reaches us in our deepest moment of need.

Psalm 91:4b also tells us that God's faithfulness is our *bulwark*. According to *Nelson's Bible Dictionary*, "*a bulwark is a tower built along a city wall from which defenders shoot arrows and hurl large stones at the enemy.*" Think about that! From that tower, God is faithful to point out the enemy so he can't sneak up on our blind side. Note that this verse declares God's faithfulness to us as both a shield and a bulwark in a two-layered analogy. The passage is using two images of fortification and protection. God is our tower—our wall of protection in a collective sense; and He is our shield—a very personal and individualized defense. This verse indicates *double* protection.

Chapter 6

I Will Not Fear The Terror

You will not be afraid of *the terror by night...* –Psalm 91:5a

IT IS INTERESTING TO note that verses five and six of Psalm 91 cover an entire 24 hour period emphasizing *day and night* protection. But, what is more important is that these two verses encompass **every evil known to man.**

The psalmist divides the list into four categories. We will look at those categories one at a time, chapter by chapter. The first—***terror by night***— includes all the evils that come through man: kidnapping, robbery, rape, murder, terrorism, wars…! It is the dread—or horror—or alarm that comes from what man can do to you. God is saying, *"You will not be afraid of any of those things…because they will not approach you" (Psalm 91:5-7).* The first thing verse five deals with is *fear.*

Never before in our history has there been so much talk of *terrorism* and *germ warfare,* but to the surprise of so many people, God is not shocked or caught off guard by these things. Do we think *chemical warfare* is bigger than God? Long before man ever discovered biological weapons, God had made provision for the protection of His people—if they would believe His Word.

> *These signs will accompany those who have believed... if they drink any deadly poison, it will not hurt them.* —Mark 16:17-18

According to the **Strong's Concordance**, the word *drink* in this Scripture comes from the Greek word *imbibe* which means "to drink, to absorb, to inhale or to take into the mind." No evil has been conceived by man against which God has not provided a promise of protection for any of his children who will choose to believe and act on it.

What about the fear that has come on mankind regarding our polluted water supplies, foods contaminated by pesticides...? I believe the Word of God advocates using wisdom, but all the precautions in the world cannot protect us from every harmful thing that could be in our food and water. Therefore, God's instruction to bless our food and water before eating is not merely some ritual to make us look more spiritual. Rather, it is another provision for our safety, playing an important role in God's protective plan.

But the Spirit explicitly says that in later times...men will advocate abstaining from food, which God has created to be gratefully shared in by those who believe and know the truth. For everything created by God is good, and nothing is to be rejected, if it is received with gratitude; for it is sanctified by means of the Word of God and prayer.
—I Timothy 4:1-5

But you shall serve the Lord your God, and He will bless your bread and your water; and He will remove sickness from your midst.
—Exodus 23:25

It is the goodness of God that He made provision before we ever asked! This is not for everyone; it is for those who *know and believe the truth.* Blessing the food with gratitude literally brings about sanctification—a cleansing of our food and water.

Over and over Jesus told us, "Do not fear!" Why do you think He continually reminds us not to be afraid? Because it is through faith in His Word that we are protected—and since fear is the opposite of faith, the Lord knows fear will keep us from operating in the faith that is necessary to receive. It is no wonder God addresses *the fear of terror* first.

So, how do we keep from being afraid? Very simply! Fear comes when we think we are responsible for bringing about this protection ourselves. Too often, we think—

"Oh, if I can just believe hard enough, maybe I'll be protected!" That's wrong thinking! The protection is already there. It has already been provided, whether we receive it or not. Faith is simply the **choice to receive** what Jesus has *already* done. The Bible has classic examples of how to deal with fear.

The answer is in the *Blood of Jesus.* Exodus 12:23 tells us when Israel put blood on the door facings, the destroyer could not come in. The animal blood they used then serves as a *type and shadow,* or a picture, of the Blood of Jesus which ratifies our *better* protection—under our *better* Covenant.

When we confess out loud, "*I am protected by the Blood of Jesus*"—and believe it, the devil literally cannot come in! Remember verse two tells us, "*I will say ... the Lord is my Refuge and my Fortress.*" It is *heart and mouth*—believing with our heart and confessing with our mouth.

Our physical weapons are operated with our hands, but we operate our *spiritual* weapons with our mouths. The Blood is applied by *saying it* in faith. Confessing with our mouth and believing with our heart starts with the new birth experience and sets precedence for receiving all of God's good gifts (Romans 10:9-10).

If we find ourselves being afraid of the *terror by night,* that is our barometer to let us know we are not dwelling and abiding up close to the Lord in the shelter of the Most

High and believing His promises. Fear comes in when we are confessing things other than what God has said. When our eyes are not on God, fear will come. But let that fear be a reminder to repent.

We walk by faith, not by sight. —2 Corinthians 5:7

We have to choose to believe His Word more than we believe what we see—more than we believe the terror attack. Not that we deny the existence of the attack. The attack may be very real, but God wants our faith in His Word to become more of a reality to us than what we see in the natural.

For example: Gravity is a fact! No one denies the existence of gravity, but just as the law of aerodynamics can supersede the law of gravity, Satan's attacks can also be superseded by a higher law—the law of faith and obedience to God's Word. Faith does not deny the existence of *terror*. There are simply higher laws in the Bible for overcoming it.

David did not deny the existence of the giant. Fear has us compare the size of the giant to ourselves. Faith, on the other hand, had David compare the size of the giant to the size of his God. David's eyes saw *the giant*, but his faith saw *the promises* (I Samuel 17).

Our daughter had a friend, Julee, living in an apartment in Ft Worth, Texas. She was getting ready for church one Sunday morning when someone knocked on her door. Never dreaming it wasn't someone she knew, she opened the door, only to be almost knocked over by a strange man who shoved his way in and attacked her.

Julee started using the Word of God as her defense. In the natural there was no way for a young girl to escape from a strong man, but confidence in her God allowed her not to give up!

It took forty-five minutes of spiritual battle as he came at her time after time. But, her persistence in quoting these words out of Psalm 91 brought confusion & immobility on him, thwarting every attempted attack. And, during one of those times when he was at a standstill, she was able to get out the door and escape unharmed.

Later, after he was apprehended and held in custody, she found out he had sexually assaulted numerous young women, and she was the only one of his victims who had been able to escape without harm. We do not have to be afraid of the terror *of what man can do to harm us.* Praise God for our higher law! God's laws triumph over man's laws.

Chapter 7

I Will Not Fear The Arrow

You will not be afraid of ... *the arrow* that flies by day.
—Psalm 91:5b

T HE SECOND CATEGORY OF evil is the *arrow that flies by day.* An arrow is something that pierces or wounds spiritually, physically, mentally or emotionally. This category indicates that you are in a spiritual battle zone—specific enemy assignments that are directed toward your life to defeat you.

Arrows are deliberately sent by the enemy and meticulously aimed at the spot that will cause the most damage. They are targeted toward the area where our mind is not renewed by the Word of God—perhaps an area where we are still losing our temper, or an area where we are still easily offended, or perhaps, an area of rebellion or fear!

Seldom does the enemy attack us in an area where we are built up and strong. He attacks us where we're still struggling. That's why we have to run to God! And when we do battle using our spiritual weapons, his arrows will not approach us.

God tells us in Ephesians 6:12 that we have a *"shield of faith to extinguish all the **flaming** darts of the enemy."* These are not just plain arrows, they are "on fire". And, God doesn't say we can miss most of them. He says that we can extinguish *"all"* of them. When arrows are sent to wound us spiritually, physically, emotionally or financially, God wants us to ask and believe by faith that He *will pick us up out of harm's way* and deliver us from calamity.

Long before my husband and I moved full time in the ministry, we owned and operated a soft drink bottling plant that his dad had started the year before Jack was born. Several years before we sold the business, one of the other bottling plants in our area changed management, and the new manager told us he was going to *spare no expense* in putting us out of business.

He told the truth! We could never have anticipated how much money he was going to spend trying to fulfill his promise. He literally went all over town, placing free vending machines wherever our venders were located, and storeowners were continually calling us to come and pick up our equipment. Financially, there was no way to compete, especially when the manager also started product price-cutting and flooding the market with advertising. The outlook in the natural was pretty dismal, but, we had something he didn't have. We had a *covenant* with God, telling us *not to be afraid of the arrow that flies by day.*

And, God is faithful. Those arrows—or circumstances— that had looked impossible for us to overcome, finally passed, and our business was left standing long after the competition was gone. The competitor had obviously expected our business to fold quickly under the intense financial pressure, but, when we were able to survive longer than he anticipated, it was *he* who went under financially.

We have a covenant with God telling us not to be afraid of the arrow that flies by day. Assignments will rise up, but don't be afraid. He has promised to protect us and He has promised the arrows will not hit their target.

Chapter 8

I Will Not Fear Pestilence

You will not be afraid of the *pestilence* that stalks in
darkness.   –Psalm 91:6a

EAR GRIPPED MY HEART and beads of perspiration
popped out on my forehead as I feverishly ran my fingers
over what felt like a lump in my body. How I dreaded that
monthly self-examination the doctor had suggested. My
fingertips were as cold as ice from the panic I had worked
up just thinking about what I might find, and the turn my
life would take from there.

On that particular day it turned out to be a false alarm,
but the dread of what I might find in the coming months
was constantly in the back of my mind until this promise
came alive in my heart.   If you fight fears of fatal diseases,
then this is the Scripture for you to take hold of.

The third category of evil that God names is **pestilence.**
This is the only evil He names twice! Since God doesn't

waste words, He must have a specific reason for repeating this promise.

Have you noticed when a person says something more than once, it is usually because he wants to emphasize a point? God knew the pestilence and the fear that would be running rampant in these end days. The world is teeming with fatal epidemics that are hitting people by the thousands, so God catches our attention by repeating this promise.

It's as though God is saying, "I said it in verse three, *but did you really hear Me?* Just to be sure, I am saying it again in verse six—*you do not have to be afraid of the deadly pestilence!*" This is so contrary to the world in which we live that we have to renew our thinking before we can comprehend the fact we do not have to be afraid of the sicknesses and diseases that are epidemic in the world today.

When I first started studying this psalm, I remember thinking, *"I don't know whether I have the faith to believe these promises!"* This thought stretched my faith and my mind until I thought it would snap like a rubber band that was being pulled too tightly.

God, however, reminded me that faith is not a feeling. Faith is simply *choosing* to believe what He says in His Word.

The more I chose to believe God's Word, the more I had a *knowing* I could trust and rely on it completely.

> *Heaven and earth will pass away, but My Words will not pass away.* —Mark 13:31

Our inheritance is not limited to what is handed down to us genetically from our ancestors. Our inheritance can be what Jesus provided for us if we believe the Word and put it to work.

> *Christ redeemed us from the curse of the law having become a curse for us...* —Galatians 3:13

The pestilence mentioned here in Psalm 91 is spelled out in detail in Deuteronomy 28. This scripture in Galatians tells us we are *redeemed* from every curse (including pestilence), if we will simply believe and appropriate the promise.

In Bible days when they mentioned pestilence, they were thinking of diseases like leprosy. Luke 21:11 states that part of the signs of the end times is an outbreak of pestilence. And, today we have many widespread diseases such as AIDS, cancer, heart disease... But, no matter what pestilence we might be facing, His promise never ceases to be true. The enemy may try to cause sudden surprises to catch us unaware and knock us down, but God is faithful. His Word is true no matter what the circumstances look like. I shudder to think what we might open ourselves up to without the promise of Psalm 91 and without the determination to stand firm and refuse to entertain fearful thoughts.

I wish I had kept a diary through the years of the healing miracles that I have seen personally. I remember the night our son was born and we were told he had a lung disease and could not be taken out of the incubator, even to be fed. After we got over the initial shock, God seemed to just drop faith in our hearts and there was never another question in our minds whether or not he would be normal. Two perfectly healthy lungs demonstrated God's healing power.

I remember when Mary Ann, a friend of mine with three incurable diseases, was practically carried into one of my Bible study meetings and laid on the couch. Her little eighty-seven pound body looked beyond hope, but the group prayers that morning incited a miracle and thirty years later she still lives. She often shows the picture on her old driver's license to illustrate the shocking difference in her appearance.

I remember the night that a member of the staff at the Texas Youth Commission approached my husband and daughter. He had been listening to their Bible studies each Monday night and wanted prayer. Two tests showed his unborn child to have Down's syndrome, but he and his wife had chosen against the recommendation to have the baby aborted and just wanted Jack and Angie to pray for them as parents. Instead, they asked if they could pray that God would bring forth a miracle. Several months later his wife gave birth to a completely whole and healthy baby. Time and space prevents my sharing all the wonderful miracles I have witnessed through the years—some instantaneous, some through a miracle process, but all brought about by the hand of God.

What we allow our mind to dwell on is *our* choice. Therefore, if we desire to operate in this protection covenant, taking authority over negative thoughts and emotions is imperative. It is amazing how the simple phrase, "*I am just not going there,*" will dispel those fears immediately.

I'm sure this promise of protection from plagues and pestilence reminds you of Israel's complete immunity from the Egyptian plagues in the land of Goshen. The destroyer could not come in where the blood was applied. The Bible claims that over one million people in the wilderness did not get sick. Even before the completed work on the cross, the Old Testament covenant declared, "*You will not be afraid of the pestilence that stalks in darkness—it will not approach you.*"

Chapter 9

I Will Not Fear Destruction

You will not be afraid of the *destruction* that lays waste at noon. —Psalm 91:6b

THIS FOURTH CATEGORY OF evil is **destruction**. Destruction takes in the *evils over which mankind has no control*—those things that the world ignorantly calls *acts of God*: tornadoes, floods, hurricanes, fire…! God very plainly tells us that we are not to fear destruction. These natural disasters are not coming from God.

In Mark 4:39, Jesus rebuked the storm and it became perfectly calm, demonstrating that God is not the author of such things—otherwise, Jesus would never have contradicted His Father by rebuking something sent by Him.

There is no place in the physical world where you can go and be safe from every *destruction*--every natural disaster. We can never anticipate what might come when we least expect it. But, no matter where you are in the world, God says to run to His shelter where *you will not be afraid of the destruction…it will not approach you!*

Late one night, soon after building our new home in the country, we were faced with a severe weather alert. The local radio station was warning that a tornado had been sited just south of the country club—the exact location of our property. We could see several of the React Club vehicles parked on the road below our hill as the members watched the funnel cloud that seemed to be headed straight for our house.

I had never seen such a strange, eerie color in the night sky or experienced such a deafening silence in the atmosphere. You could literally feel the hair on your body standing on end. Some of our son's friends were visiting, and, to their surprise, Jack quickly ordered our family to get outside with our Bibles and start circling the house— reading Psalm 91 and taking authority. Jack had the children out speaking directly to the storm, just like Jesus did.

The weird silence suddenly turned into a roar, with torrents of rain coming down in what seemed like bucketfuls, rather than drops. Finally, Jack got a peace that the danger had passed, even though by sight nothing had changed.

We walked back into the house just in time to hear the on-location radio announcer exclaim with so much excitement that he was almost shouting, *"This is nothing short of a miracle—the funnel cloud south of the Brownwood Country Club has suddenly lifted back in the sky and vanished before our very eyes."*

You should have seen those kids jumping and hollering. It was the friends' first time to observe the supernatural at work. Their surprise, however, was no greater than that of the professor the next day when he asked the students what they were doing during the storm. Several said that they were in the bathtub under a mattress—some were in closets and one was in a storm cellar!

You can imagine the astonishment when he got around to our daughter, Angelia, who said, "With the tornado headed our direction, my family was circling the house, quoting from Psalm 91—we *will not be afraid of the destruction that lays waste…it will not approach us."*

***

DID YOU KNOW THAT EVERY EXTREME EVIL KNOWN TO MAN WILL FALL INTO ONE OF THESE FOUR CATEGORIES THAT WE HAVE NAMED IN CHAPTERS SIX THROUGH NINE (Verses 5-6): TERROR, ARROWS, PESTILENCE, OR DESTRUCTION? AND THE AMAZING THING IS THAT GOD HAS OFFERED US DELIVERANCE FROM THEM ALL!

God lets us know in Psalm 91, *"You will not be afraid of* **terror**, **arrows**, **pestilence** *or* **destruction** *because I have said in*

*My Word that **it will not approach you**—if you are obedient to verses one and two to dwell in My shelter and abide in My shadow."* And, of course, we cannot dwell and abide in Him apart from Jesus. But, praise God!—because of the shed Blood of the Cross, it has now been made possible.

We can receive anything that God has already provided. The secret is knowing that *everything for which God has made provision* is clearly spelled out and defined in the Word of God. **If you can find where God has offered it— you can have it!** It is never God holding it back. His provision is already there—waiting to be received.

Faith is not a tool to manipulate God into giving you something *you* want. Faith is simply the means by which we accept what God has already made available.

Our goal needs to be the *renewal* of our minds, to such an extent that we have more faith in God's Word than in what we see. God does not make promises that are out of our reach.

When the Lord first began showing me these promises and my mind was struggling with doubt, He took me to a portion of His Word that helped to set me free.

What then! If some did not believe, their unbelief will not nullify the faithfulness of God, will it! May it never be! Rather, let God be found true, though every man be found a liar, as it is written: that thou mightiest prevail when thou art judged.
—Romans 3:3-4

God is telling us that, even though there may be some who don't believe, their unbelief will never nullify His promises to the ones who do believe. A very important part of that verse in Romans 3 is the reminder, in a quote from the Old Testament, that what we as individuals choose to believe and confess will determine our own individual judgment.

Without the promises of protection throughout the Word of God, and especially, without our Psalm 91 covenant— listing all of the protection promises in one chapter—we might feel rather presumptuous, if, on our own, we prayed *asking* God to protect us from all the things covered in these four categories. In fact, we probably would not have the nerve to ask for all of that, but God is so good. **He offered this protection to us before we even had a chance to ask!** It was God's plan to provide protection for His children, even before the foundation of the world.

Chapter 10

Though a Thousand Fall

A thousand may fall at your side and ten thousand at your right hand, but it shall not approach you.   —Psalm 91:7

D O WE EVER STOP to consider what this is saying to us? Do we have the courage to trust God's Word enough to believe **that He means this literally?** And, is it possible for it to be true, and yet still miss out on these promises? Jesus answers the last question in Luke 4:27, *"There were many lepers in Israel in the time of Elijah, but none of them was cleansed."* Only Naaman, the Syrian, was healed when he obeyed in faith. **Not everyone will receive the benefits of this promise in Psalm 91.** Only those who believe God and hold fast to His promises will profit; none-the-less, it *is* available. And to the measure we trust Him, we will in the same measure reap the benefits of that trust.

What an awesome statement! God wants us to know that even though there will be a thousand falling by our side and ten thousand at our right hand, it does not negate the promise that destruction will not approach the one who chooses to believe and trust His Word. The *Amplified Bible* says, "...*it shall not approach you **for any purpose**"* (emphasis added). He means exactly what He says.

It is no accident that this little statement is tucked right here in the middle of the psalm. Have you noticed how easy it is to become fearful when disaster starts striking all around you? We begin to feel like Peter must have felt as he walked on the water to Jesus. It is easy to see how he started sinking with the waves when he saw all the turbulence of the storm going on around him.

God knew there would be times when we would hear so many negative reports, see so many needs and encounter so much danger around us that we would feel overwhelmed. That is why He warned us ahead of time that *thousands would be falling all around us.* He didn't want us to be caught off guard. But, at that point, we have a choice to make. The ball is then in our court! We can either choose to run to His shelter in faith and it will not approach us or we can passively live our lives the way the world does, not realizing there is something we can do about it.

What tremendous insight, after our minds have been renewed by the Word of God, to realize, contrary to the world's thinking, that we do not have to be among *the ten thousand who fall at our right hand.*

Psalm 91 is the *preventive* **measure that God has given to His children against every evil known to mankind.** No place else in the Word are all of the protection promises (including help from angels, as well as promises insuring our authority) accumulated in one covenant to offer such a total package for living in this world. It is both an *offensive* and *defensive measure* to ward off every evil before it has had time to strike. This is not only a *cure,* but a plan for *complete prevention!*

A year after Hurricane Ivan hit, Jack and I stayed in the beach home of our friends, John and Virginia Loyd in Orange Beach, Alabama. For one week we just drove through the area, appalled at the devastation we saw—even after that many months of repairs had taken place. A stone's throw from their house all the decking at the public boat docks, the gigantic dry dock building, and the restaurant glass had all been blown away. What was left of the marina building was under three feet of water. On the other side of the house we saw what once was a shopping center had been reduced to a pile of rubble. Condos and hotels were completely gutted. Even after that length of time, mounds of siding and roofing shingles from the homes next to our friends' beach house still littered the adjacent properties.

Only after seeing the destruction with our own eyes did we realize the supernatural protection the Loyds had received. Prior to and during the hurricane the year before, they had called us declaring their total trust in the Lord's Psalm 91 covenant promise of protection and getting us to join in faith with them. **When they returned to the area there was NO damage to their beach house or property.** When a hurricane passes over, flooding brings much of the destruction because the water goes everywhere. Only God knows how He kept the water out of their beach home! **THE WORD WORKS!** And, did I mention that at the time, the Loyds also owned a beach front condo just three blocks away that was up for sale. In spite of the fact that the condo was directly on the ocean, when John opened the door to the condo not even a picture on the wall had been disturbed nor was the (NOT covered with plywood) patio glass broken. Yet, the eye of Hurricane Ivan had gone directly over the top of their building. Coincidence? If you had driven down Beach Rd (even a year later, when we did) you would know that it was nothing but the power of God's protection that had shielded them. Praise God! Psalm 91 is not limited to areas where hurricanes can't reach. We can even be immune in the midst of mass destruction.

You will only look on with your eyes, and see the
recompense of the wicked.   –Psalm 91:8

You will see recompense (payment) being doled out at times. There is judgment. There is justice. Every sin will be exposed sooner or later and paid for. An evil dictator falls, an unrighteous aggressor is stopped, a tyrant faces his crimes against humanity, a wrong is rectified—*the recompense of the wicked speaks of justice.* Wars have been fought where one side had a righteous cause, and eventually, good won over evil. The justness of God is that evil will not triumph—that Hitlers do not win—that communistic governments fall—that darkness does not extinguish light.

This verse says that we will "*only look on and see*" it happening. The word "only" denotes a protection of only seeing and not experiencing the evil; and it denotes detachment in that the evil we see does not get inside of us. We are set apart in that we do not allow our enemy's hate to change us.

Let's look for just a moment at this Scripture with our faith in mind. Do we sometimes fall short into unbelief? Faith in God, in His Son Jesus Christ and in His Word is *counted* in God's eyes as righteousness. But, when we are in unbelief, to a degree we are placing ourselves in the category of the *wicked*. Sometimes, even as a Christian, I have been an *unbelieving* believer when it comes to receiving *all* of God's Word. Jesus says in Matthew 5:18,

"Not the smallest letter or stroke of His Word will pass away until it is all accomplished." Even if believers have never utilized this psalm in its full potential the truth has never passed away or lost one ounce of its power.

Many people think of the Gospel as an insurance policy, securing only their eternity and their comfort after disaster strikes. They are depriving themselves of so much. Perhaps, we all need to ask ourselves the question, *"What kind of coverage do I have—fire or life?"* God's Word is more than just an escape from Hell; it is a handbook for living a victorious *life* in this world.

There is a difference, however, between the destruction that comes from the enemy and persecution for the Gospel's sake. II Timothy 3:12 tells us, *"all who desire to live godly in Christ Jesus will be persecuted."* There are times when we will be mistreated because of our stand for the cause of Christ. But, persecution for living a Godly life is totally different from the evil talked about in Psalm 91. Psalm 91 is not dealing with persecution. Jesus suffered persecution, but He did not have calamity, disaster and mishap. Accidents never even approached Him.

A thousand may fall at your side and ten thousand at your right hand, but it shall not approach you... for you have made the Lord, my refuge, even the Most High, your dwelling place. –Psalm 91:9

Have you ever been in spiritual warfare where it seemed that everyone was falling around you? If this verse isn't a description of actual combat, I don't know what is—yet, tied to it is a promise of protection beyond anything that can be envisioned. There is a place where calamity literally does not even approach us. This concept is hard to imagine in a peaceful season of life—yet, how much more remarkable is this promise when it's given in connection with the spiritual battle described above. The portrayal of people falling is directly connected to the promise that it will *not even come near us.* Two opposite poles joined together! This psalm is making its strongest offer of protection right in the midst of chaos. And, it is a type of protection that stands in a category all its own.

Too many people see Psalm 91 as a beautiful promise that they file right alongside all of their other good quality reading material and it makes them feel comforted every time they read it. But, I do not want anyone to read this book and fail to see the *superior significance* to these promises in this psalm. These are not written for our inspiration, but for our protection. These are not words of comfort *in* affliction, but words of deliverance *from* affliction.

Chapter 11

No evil will befall you, nor will any plague or calamity come near your dwelling. —Psalm 91:10

ARE YOU WORRIED ABOUT your family? This part of Psalm 91 is written in capital letters just for you. After God repeats our part of the condition in verse nine, He then re-emphasizes the promise in verse ten: " ...*nor will it come near your dwelling place (your household).*" It is at this point in the psalm that the Bible makes this covenant more comprehensive than just being about ourselves!

God has just *added a new dimension* to the promise: the opportunity to exercise faith, not only for ourselves, but also for the protection of our entire household. If these promises were only available to us as individuals, it would not be very comforting. Because God has created within us both an instinct to be protected and a need to protect those who belong to us, He has assured us here that these promises are for you ***and your household***.

It appears that the Old Testament leaders had a better understanding of this concept than we who are under the New Covenant. That is why Joshua chose for himself *and for his household*.

> *If it is disagreeable in your sight to serve the Lord, then choose for yourselves today whom you will serve; but as for me **and my house**, we will serve the Lord.* —Joshua 24:15

As Joshua made the decision that his household would serve God with him, he was influencing their destiny and declaring their protection at the same time. In much the same way, Rahab bargained with the Israeli spies for her whole family (Joshua 2:13).

When our hearts are truly steadfast and when we are trusting in His faithfulness to fulfill His promises, we'll not be constantly afraid that something bad is going to happen to one of our family members.

> *You will not be afraid of evil tidings because your heart is steadfast—trusting in His Word.*
> —Psalm 112:7

Negative expectations will begin to pass away, and we will start expecting good reports. According to this verse, we can grab our ears and proclaim, "These ears were made to hear good tidings." The fear of bad tidings can plague our very existence. That fear of the phone ringing in the night, of that knock on the door, or of the siren of an ambulance… this is the verse that gives the promise that a steadfast heart will not live in constant fear of tragic news. Someone once said, "Fear knocked, faith answered, and no one was there." When fear knocks, let your mouth say this verse out loud, *"I will not fear evil tidings, my heart is steady, trusting in you!"*

Several years ago as I was cooking breakfast, Jack walked into the kitchen with one of the glands under his chin so swollen that it looked as though he had attempted to swallow a large soft ball that had lodged on one side of his throat. I rushed him to this close physician friend of ours, and I thought I could tell by the expression on the doctor's face that he was concerned. But, when the first words out of his mouth were, *"I am going to call in another doctor to have a look at you,"* my worst fear was confirmed, and, I then knew he was suspecting that there was something seriously wrong.

At that point, the enemy tried to unload a whole carload of fear thoughts and fear pictures in my mind, but when God's Word has been stored in the heart, it has a way of surfacing just when it's needed. This Scripture in *Psalm 91: 10:* "No evil will befall you, nor will any plague or calamity *come near your dwelling"* was more than just a *comforting* thought. It brought *life* and *hope* to the situation.

I sat there in the waiting room, thanking God for this promise and rejoicing over the outcome long before the doctor ever poked his smiling face around the corner to tell me that everything was fine. It turned out to be just a sore throat that had settled in the gland on one side of Jack's throat. Even the swelling had gone down by the next morning. It is so rewarding to have Psalm 91 promises that include more than just our own life. It is a family that is under that umbrella of protection, based on the extension of this promise in verse ten that moves us from just the individual to the household.

In Matthew 13:32, Jesus makes reference to a mustard seed starting as an herb but growing into a tree with birds nesting in the branches. Others can find protection in our faith, as well, when we plant the seed of the Word.

Towns are one big collection of families, and family protection could not have been more clearly demonstrated than by what took place in Seadrift, Texas, during WWII. The town's citizens decided to pray Psalm 91 collectively over every one of their husbands, sons, grandsons, cousins, uncles and friends who were going to war. A bulletin board was made with photos of every service man and a commitment made that every single day intercessors would cover them in prayer. Every time they met they would read from Psalm 91.

It seemed that everyone had a family member who had gone to fight. What a testimony to this promise of family protection when every single man returned safely home from war—from all over the world. THIS TOWN DID NOT SUFFER A SINGLE COMBAT CASUALTY while so many other towns and families experienced much grief and heartache, and often, multiple casualties.

The beauty of this psalm is that when someone prays for more than himself, he brings the entire family under a shield of God's Word. It is an added dimension to us as individuals to be able to apply the richness of this covenant to our entire household. What a joy to know you have promises in Psalm 91 that will not only protect you, but also those in your family and *near your dwelling*.

I thank God for this added dimension of being able to apply *His Covenant Umbrella of Protection* for your entire household. What a joy to know that your family is safe.

Chapter 12

Angels Watching Over Me

For He will give His angels charge concerning you, to guard you in all your ways. They will bear you up in their hands, lest you strike your foot against a stone. —Psalm 91:11-12

IN VERSES ELEVEN AND twelve God makes another unique promise concerning an additional dimension of our protection. This is one of the most precious promises of God, and He put it right here in Psalm 91. In fact, this is one of the promises Satan used to test Jesus on the Mount of Temptation.

Most Christians read past this promise with very little, if any, thought about the magnitude of what is being said. Only after we get to Heaven will we realize all the things from which we were spared because of the intervention of God's angels on our behalf.

I am sure you have read stories about missionaries whose lives were spared because would-be murderers saw large bodyguards protecting them—when, in fact, there was no one there in the natural. And, we can all recall close calls where we escaped a tragedy, and there was no explanation in the natural. It is possible *"to entertain angels without knowing it"* as it says in Hebrews 13:2, but sadly, I believe most Christians have a tendency to disregard the ministry of angels altogether.

Floyd, a friend of ours who was working in the mines in Clovis, New Mexico, had the responsibility of setting off the explosives. One particular day he was ready to push the switch when someone tapped him on the shoulder. To his surprise no one was anywhere around. Deciding that it must have been his imagination, he started once again to detonate the explosion when he felt another tap on his shoulder. Again, no one was there, so he decided to move all the ignition equipment several hundred feet back up the tunnel. When he finally plunged the charger, the whole top of the tunnel caved in exactly where he had been standing. A coincidence? You could never make our friend believe that. He knew *someone* had tapped him on the shoulder.

This verse 11 says, *"For He will give His angels charge concerning you!"* What does that mean? Think with me for a moment! Have you ever *taken charge* of a situation? When you take charge of something, you put yourself in a place of leadership. You begin telling everyone what to do and how to do it. If angels are taking charge of the things that concern us, God has given the angels, **not the circumstances**, the authority to act on our behalf. That same truth is repeated in Hebrews.

Are they (angels) not all ministering spirits, sent out to render service for the sake of those who will inherit salvation?　　　　—Hebrews 1:14

Have you ever been fishing on a lake in the middle of the night? Some people think that is the very best time to catch fish. When my husband was seven years old, all the people who worked for his father took their boats to Lake Brownwood to do some night fishing. Jack was placed in a boat with five adults so he would be well supervised. Since one of the men in the boat was an expert swimmer, his mother and dad thought he would be in especially good hands.

Later that night during one of the times when the boats were going back and forth to shore for bait, Jack had gotten out of his boat and into another one without anyone noticing. Then, off they went—without Jack—back onto the lake in the dark. This was back before there were rules about life jackets and lights on your fishing boats, so no one could see in the dark what actually happened. Perhaps, they hit a stump, but for some reason the boat Jack had been in sank. All five of the people in it drowned, including the expert swimmer. It became obvious that Jack had been directed to another boat by *angels who serve God and are sent to help those who will receive salvation.*

When we look to God as the Source of *our* protection and provision, the angels are constantly *rendering us aid* and *taking charge* of our affairs. Psalm 103:20 says, *"His angels mighty in strength… obey the voice of His Word."* As we proclaim God's Word, the angels hasten to carry it out.

Verse eleven also says *"Angels will guard you in all your ways."* Have you ever seen a soldier standing guard, protecting someone? That soldier stands at attention: alert, watchful and ready to protect at the first sign of attack. How much more will God's angels stand *guard* over God's children, alert and ready to protect them at all times? Do we believe that? Have we ever even thought about it? Faith is what releases this promise to work in our behalf. How comforting it is to know that God has placed these heavenly guards to have charge over us.

Psalm 91 names so many different avenues through which God protects us. It is exciting to realize from this Old Testament psalm that protection is not just an idea in God's Mind—He is committed to it. Angelic protection is just another one of the *unique* ways in which God has provided that protection. What an unusual idea to add actual beings designed to protect us. He charged angels *to guard us in all our ways.*

Chapter 13

The Enemy Under My Feet

> You will tread upon the lion and cobra, the young lion and the serpent (*dragon* in the KJV) you will trample down.
> —Psalm 91:13

HERE IN VERSE THIRTEEN God transitions to another topic. He takes us from the subject of our being protected *by Him,* and puts emphasis on *the authority in His Name* that has been given to us as believers. Make a note of the corresponding New Testament Scripture that deals with the authority that has been given to us:

> *Behold, I [Jesus] have given you authority to tread upon serpents and scorpions, and over all the power of the enemy, and nothing shall injure you.*
> —Luke 10:19

We, as Christians, have been given authority over the enemy. H*e does not have authority over us!* We need to take the time to allow that fact to soak in! However, our authority over the enemy is not automatic.

My husband says that too many Christians *take authority* when they should be *praying*, and they *pray* when they should be *taking authority*! For the most part Jesus prayed at night and took authority all day. When we encounter the enemy—that is not the time to start praying. We need to be already "prayed up". When we encounter the enemy, we need to be speaking forth the authority that we have in the Name of Jesus.

If a gunman suddenly faced you, would you be confident enough in your authority that you could boldly declare, *"I am in Covenant with the Living God, and I have a Blood Covering that protects me from anything that you might attempt to do. So, in the Name of Jesus, I command you to put down that gun!"*?

If we do not have that kind of courage, then we need to meditate on the authority Scriptures until we become confident in who we are *in Christ*. At new birth we immediately have enough power placed at our disposal to tread upon the enemy without being harmed. Most Christians, however, either do not know it, or they fail to use it. How often do we believe the Word enough to act on it?

Now, let's look at what this verse is actually saying. What good does it do to have authority over lions and cobras unless we are in Africa or India or some exotic place like that? What **does** the Word mean when it says, "W*e will tread on the lion, the young lion, the cobra, and the dragon?*" This is a graphic illustration of things that are potentially harmful in our daily lives. These terms are just an unforgettable means of describing the different types of satanic oppression that come against us. So, what do these terms mean to us today? Let's break them down...

First of all, there are **"lion problems"** — those problems that are bold, loud and forthright — problems that come out in the open and hit us face on. At one time or another we have all had something come against us that was blatant and overt. It might have been a car wreck or a boss who chewed us out royally in front of our fellow employees. Or, it might have been an unexpected bill at the end of the month that caused a chain reaction of checks bouncing. Those are *lion* problems—obvious difficulties that often seem insurmountable. Yet, God says that we will tread on them—they will not tread on us.

The **"young lions"** can grow into full-grown problems if we don't handle them. These young lion problems come against us to harass and destroy gradually, like little foxes. Subtle negative thoughts that tell us we will not survive or that our spouse no longer loves us or that we are no longer in love with our mate are good examples of this category. And, those little foxes will grow into big ones if they are not taken captive and destroyed (2 Corinthians 10:4-5). Answer those little foxes with the Word of God. Small harassments, distractions and irritations are young lions.

Catch the foxes for us, the little foxes that are ruining the vineyards, while our vineyards are in blossom.
                                    –Song of Solomon 2:15

Next, God names **"cobra"** problems. These are the problems that seem to sneak up on us like a *snake in the grass* throughout our day, while minding our own business. They are what we might call an *undercover* attack that brings sudden death—a deceptive scheme that keeps us blinded until it devours us.

How many times have you witnessed an unexpected church split or a marriage that fell apart so suddenly that you couldn't imagine what had happened—only to find out later that there had been offenses, gossip, and undermining of authority going on behind the scenes? By the time the cause was uncovered, the poison had had its effect on its victims. Puncture wounds from fangs are hard to detect, and no one sees the poison as it travels through a body, but the results are always damaging, and, oftentimes, deadly. We definitely need God's protection from *cobra* attacks.

The previous figurative examples we might have guessed, but what are the "**dragon**" problems? I looked up that Hebrew word in the *Strong's Concordance* and it listed "*sea monster*." First of all, there is no such thing as a dragon or a sea monster. Dragons are a figment of one's imagination. But, have you ever experienced fears that were a figment of your imagination? Sure you have! We all have!

Dragon problems represent our unfounded fears—phantom fears or mirage fears. That sounds harmless enough, but are you aware that phantom fears can be as deadly as the reality fears—if we believe them?

Some people's *dragon* fears are as real to them as another person's *lion* problems. That is why it is important to define your fears. So many people spend all of their lives running from something that is not even chasing them.

The wicked flee when no one is pursuing...
–Proverbs 28:1

This verse is a good definition of phantom fears. We have had a great many people share testimonies of God's deliverance from things like fear of the unknown, fear of the dark, fear of clowns, fear of dolls, fear of vampires, fear of facing the future alone, fear of loss, fear of death, tormenting suspicions, claustrophobia, etc.

Television and horror movies have built some very realistic imaginary fears. Fantasy fears can cause us to do a lot of unnecessary running in life, so authority over *dragons* is not a mental game.

But the *Good News* is—God says that we will tread on *all* of the powers of the enemy — no matter how loud and bold, sneaky and deceptive or imaginary the fears may be. God has given us authority over all of them!

No longer are we to put up with the paralyzing fears that, at one time, gripped our hearts and left us powerless at the sight of the evil that was striking all around us. God has given us His *Power of Attorney,* and these problems now have to submit to the authority of His Name.

The word *tread* gives us a good visionary. I think of a tank crossing a brushy plain. Where the tank treads go, everything is crushed and left flat on the ground. It is a great picture of our authority over these spiritual enemies as well, treading like a tank and crushing all that is evil in our path. That is a strong description of our authority in walking over the lion, young lion, cobra and dragon.

Chapter 14

Because I Love Him

Because he has loved Me, therefore I will... —Psalm 91:14a

IN VERSES FOURTEEN THROUGH sixteen the author of the Psalm changes from talking in third person *about* God's promises to God speaking to us personally from His *secret place* and *announcing* promises in the first person. It is a dramatic shift in tone as it moves to God speaking prophetically to each one of us directly, denoting significantly more depth in the relationship. In these three verses He gives *seven promises* with as much open triumph as a man has when a woman accepts his proposal. A commitment to love involves choice. When you pick that person out of all the others, you set your love on that one and you embark on a deeper relationship. That is the picture of how God sets His love on us. In the same way this passage challenges the reader to set his love on God. When he does, the promises come into effect and God is indulgent with His promises to the one who loves Him.

Love is the cohesiveness that binds man to God, and God will be faithful to His beloved. Love always requires presence and nearness. Special memories are birthed out of relationship. That is why this section cannot be explained, but has to be experienced. Let me give you an illustration...

If you are a parent, you may have watched in horror as your young child picked up a newly birthed kitten by the throat and carried it all over the yard. You may have wondered how it ever survived. It was an old, red hen that endured the distress dished out by our very enthusiastic children.

Ole red would allow herself to be picked up while in the process of laying her egg and deposit it right in Angie's eager, little hands. The children had some merit to what they advertised as the *freshest eggs in town*—a few times the egg never hit the nest. Nesting season had its own special fascination for the children as they watched Ole Red try to hatch out more eggs than she could sit on. The kids would number the eggs in pencil to ensure that each egg was properly rotated and kept warm. They would wait out the twenty-one days and then, with contagious delight, call me out to see the nest swarming with little ones. That ole hen had a brood of chicks that was hatched out of eggs from every hen in the henhouse.

Observing a setting hen this close had its own rare charm as one could witness the protection she gave those chicks in a way most people never have the chance to observe. I remember her feathers as she fanned them out. I remember the smell of the fresh straw the kids kept in the nest. I remember that I could see through that soft, downy underside and watch the rhythmic beating of her heart. Those chicks had an almost enviable position— something that all the books on the *theology of protection* could never explain in mere words. This was the unforgettable picture of a real life understanding of what it means to be *under the wings*. Those were some happy chicks! This lets one see in a much more intimate way that **true protection** has everything to do with ***closeness***.

Some people acknowledge that there is a God; others *know* Him. Neither maturity, nor education, nor family heritage, nor even a lifetime as a nominal Christian can make a person "*know*" Him. Only an encounter with the Lord and time spent with Him will cause one to lay hold of the promises in these verses of Psalm 91.

We need to ask ourselves, "*Do I really love Him?*" Jesus even asked this of Peter, a close disciple, *"Peter, do you love Me (John 21:15)?"* Can you imagine how Peter must have felt when Jesus questioned him three times, "*Peter, do you love Me?*" Even so, we need to question ourselves, because these promises are made only to those who have genuinely set their love on Him. Take special note of the fact that **these seven promises are *reserved* for those who return His Love.**

And, remember that the Lord said in John 14:15, *"If you love Me, you will obey Me!"* Our obedience is an extremely reliable *telltale* sign that shows us that we really love Him. *Do you love Him?* **If you do, these promises are for you!**

Chapter 15

God is My Deliverer

Because he has loved Me, therefore *I will deliver him...*
—Psalm 91: 14a

A PROMISE OF DELIVERANCE is the first of the seven promises made to the one who loves God. Make it personal! For instance, I quote it like this: *"Because I love You, Lord, I thank You that You have promised to deliver me."*

When I was young I personally needed deliverance. I almost destroyed my marriage, my family, and my reputation because I was tormented with fear. One incident opened the door. I can remember the very instant my happy life changed into a nightmare that lasted eight years. And, one verse walked me out of this living mental hell: *"All who call on the Name of the Lord shall be delivered (Joel 2:32)."* Many of you desperately need God's promise of deliverance. The Word worked for me and it will work for you.

There are also other types of deliverances. There is the internal and the external. Ask yourself, "From what is He going to deliver me?" Remember the external deliverances discussed in previous chapters.

God will deliver us from *all* of the following:

* The lion problems
* The young lion problems
* The cobra problems
* The dragon problems
* The terror by night

    (evils that come through man—

    war, terror, violence…)

* The arrows that fly by day —

    (The enemy assignments sent to wound)

* The pestilence—

    (plagues, deadly diseases, fatal epidemics)

* The destruction—

    (evils over which man has no control)

In other words, God wants to deliver us from every evil known to mankind. What a promise. I thank God that He is the God of deliverance! Deliverance is all encompassing. It happens internally and externally; in fact, it surrounds us.

Thou art my hiding place; Thou dost preserve me from trouble; Thou dost surround me with songs of deliverance. —Psalm 32:7

Nothing is impossible with God! —Luke 1:37

Chapter 16

I Am Seated With Him On High

Because he has loved Me...I will set him securely on high because he has known My Name.　　　　　—Psalm 91:14b

TO BE SET SECURELY **on high** is the second promise to those who love the Lord and know Him by Name. *What all is there to know about a name?* When God wanted to show the people something important about Himself, or about His promises in the Old Testament, He would make it known by revealing another one of His covenant Names. His Name revealed Himself: Jehovah Jireh is above lack, His Name Jehovah Rapha is higher than sickness, His Name as Jehovah Shalom is above a revved up, restless mind. We see this theme of *His Name above all other names* also in the New Testament,

> *...which He brought about in Christ, when He raised Him from the dead, and seated Him at His right hand in the heavenly places, far above all rule and authority and power and dominion and every name that is named, not only in this age, but also in the one to come... and raised us up with Him, and seated us with Him in the heavenly places, in Christ Jesus.*　　　　　—Ephesians 1:20-21; 2:6

It is interesting that God pulls us up to where He is! Things look better from higher up. Our vantage point is greatly improved when we are seated with Him on high. God's perspective from on High is, in fact, the only answer. Overwhelmed from viewing life at eye level, the concept of God's promise to lift us on High is not only a fresh perspective, but, it is in reality, the only answer that works.

The Bible often refers to the unique situation of being positioned *on high* illustrated in everything from Moses stationed at the top of the mountain (Exodus 17:8-16) to God's admonition for us to mount up on wings of eagles (Isaiah 40:31) to the command to lift up our eyes (Psalm 121:1).

Notice that this verse Psalm 91:14 uses the word *"known"*. *Do you know Him by Name?* These promises come out of a *"knowing"* relationship. This is not an "impersonal" God with whom you don't interact. This promise is connected to knowing His Name.

In the first two sentences alone, the psalmist refers to God by four different names. The writer refers to God as *The Most High,* revealing that He is the highest thing that exists. This implies much more significance when we realize we are set *securely on high* with the One who is Most High.

Secondly, in the opening of Psalm 91, God is also called *The Almighty,* denoting that He is "all" mighty—the most powerful. Next, He is referred to as *The Lord,* revealing ownership. Then, the writer calls Him *My God,* making it personal. We see God unveiled in these four unique ways to the man who has known His Name. This promise of being seated securely on high is, therefore, reserved for the one who *experiences God intimately.* God says that the promises are ours — simply, because we *know His Name.*

It might sound strange if someone said, "I serve 'High'". Yet, this is the way Psalm 91:1 first introduces His Name. God is "Most High". And, we are positionally placed with Him by dwelling and taking refuge—in our God named "The Most High." When you were a little child, did you ever go to a parade and find yourself unable to see the passing floats because of the throng of people in front of you? That happened to me once, and I remember my father picking me up and putting me on his shoulders. It was wonderful. From that high up, I was able to see the whole parade--not just what was passing right in front of me. I could look down the street and see what had already passed and what was yet to come!

This psalm has built a case for the benefits of being in the shadow of the "Most" High. Verse by verse we see what this entails. Verse 14 connects His Name to the Promise. Out of all the promises it is the only one connected to His Name. How interesting to think that "the *Most* High" *sets us* on High. This gives us the concept that the Most High pulls us up *so high* with Himself that it makes harm unable to reach us.

I will set him "securely" on high...(NASB). Besides "securely" being a good promise for those afraid of heights, there's a lot more being said. The adverb *securely* holds a lot of promise. It literally means you can't be toppled. When you are positioned securely it takes away the fear and you begin thinking and operating from a different perspective.

While traveling in Israel, I was told a story by an officer in the IDF that illustrates the superior perspective of a higher position. During the daring 1976 rescue of the hijacked Air France passengers at Entebbe, Israel was making plans to liberate the hostages instead of giving in to any demands of the PLO terrorists. One little known fact is the story of the Mossad pilot who attempted the impossible when he photographed the Entebbe airport without raising suspicion. In a bold plan, the pilot informed the control tower that he was experiencing technical difficulties, making it impossible to land. He flew in circles until he got all the photographs that the Israeli intelligence needed. The aerial photos arrived just in the nick of time as the commandos were leaving on their mission to rescue the hostages.

While we visited with an Israeli couple who were the famous "newlyweds" among the hostages, they told about the bravery of the IDF who rescued them and the shock of outside gunfire as soldiers came bursting in.

The pilot's photos gave the commandos on the ground an aerial view of the changes in the entry of the terminal that had been made since the original blueprints the Mossad had of the airport. These two testimonials illustrate the difference between viewing things from "on high" versus having just an earthly perspective. The pilot, from on high, had a view of the whole airport terminal while the hostages could only see their ranting captors with machine guns at eye level. From his elevated perspective, the pilot could see the possibility of getting to the captives, and it was from that position on high that a rescue plan was set in motion. The people trapped inside had no knowledge of the pilot circling overhead and of the planes that would soon come to rescue them. There was a lot going on *from on high* that made the difference. Let's not forget to look for our answers from a higher perspective by getting so locked into our eye-level circumstances.

Paul refers to this in Colossians...

So if you're serious about living this new resurrection life with Christ, act like it. Pursue the things over which Christ presides. Don't shuffle along, eyes to the ground, absorbed with the things right in front of you. Look up, and be alert to what is going on around Christ—that's where the action is. See things from his perspective.*

–Colossians 3:1-2 (The Message)

This unique concept resounds through the entire psalm as God makes the promise to those who **know His Name** (verse 14) that we are seated *securely* on High, *sheltered* with the Most High (verse 1), *dwelling* with Him in both a Most High home and place of safety (verse 9).

Chapter 17

God Answers My Call

He will call on Me, and *I will answer him*...

–Psalm 91:15a

GOD MAKES A THIRD promise here in verse fifteen that **He will *answer*** those who truly love Him and call on His Name. Are we aware of what a wonderful promise God is making to us here?

> *And this is the confidence which we have before Him, that, if we ask anything according to His will, He hears us. And if we know that He hears us in whatever we ask, we know that we have the requests which we have asked from Him.* –1 John 5:14-15

Nothing gives me more comfort than to realize that every time I pray in line with God's Word, He hears me. And, if He hears me, I know I have the request for which I asked. This one promise keeps me continually searching His Word in order to understand His will and His promises, so that I can know how to pray more effectively.

Sometimes I just ask God for help. When our children were teenagers, we gave them our Chevrolet Classic Impala car. To our utter surprise, the four of us came home one day to find it missing from the carport. The Sheriff department did all the necessary investigation, then, told us it was foolish to ever expect to see the car again. They were certain that by this time it was across the Mexican border with a brand new paint job.

With two teenagers we needed that second car, so we started *calling on God.* It took a little effort to do what we knew we must—to forgive our assailant and pray for him. I can't say that there was much more than a grain of mustard seed faith, but with all we could muster, we continued to call on God.

One week, to the day, after the car was missing from the carport, a young man turned himself in to the police—saying that he had stolen things all of his life, but this was the first time he had ever felt guilty. He confessed to stealing our car and told them where he had left it. Sure enough, there it was—exactly where he had said—on the parking lot of the rodeo grounds in a small town not far from Brownwood.

Sometimes we're guilty of just letting the car go and accepting what people say instead of calling on God and believing Him to answer. But, God's Word tells us that *"…whoever believes (trust) in Him will not be disappointed"* *(Romans 10:11 NASB).*

This next miracle involved our grandson, Cullen. The summer that Cullen was five years old, he was swimming with a friend and his cousins in their pool. One of the adults had said, "OK, time to get out of the pool." Everyone else had headed inside the house when Cullen saw a plastic life raft come floating by. In a flash he said to his friend, "Hey, watch this," as he stepped off the side of the pool onto the raft as though it were a solid piece. It flipped out from under him, and he fell backwards into the water, grazing his head on the side of the pool as he fell.

It was the deep end of the pool, and the friend said that he watched Cullen, with his arms and legs outstretched, just start sinking to the bottom. Quickly, he dived in and grabbed Cullen under the arms, but Cullen was unusually big for his age and weighed a great deal more than his friend. His dad always said that he felt like a chunk of lead when you tried to lift him, so the friend began to wonder if he could ever get him to the top of the water—especially since he realized he had been dazed from scraping his head on the concrete.

Realizing they were in trouble, the friend said the only thing he knew to do was to call on God, and suddenly, he said he felt someone grab him from behind and begin pushing the two of them straight up from the bottom of the pool. (The friend was sure that one of the adults had seen them and dived in to help.) In seconds, he said he shot up out of the water with Cullen above him. Then, he explained that it was like someone pulled Cullen from his arms and laid him on the side of the pool. (The friend was in water way over his head, so there was no way he could have lifted dead weight out of the pool.) Cullen started crying and coughing, and when the friend looked around, no one was there—absolutely, no one! He knew *God had heard him call,* and had sent an angel to *answer his call.*

By this time, the adults had realized something was wrong and had come running out of the house. The friend was shocked that everyone started treating him like a hero, and even gave him a plaque for saving Cullen's life. He later confessed, however, that he knew he could not have done that rescue alone. He said, "I am only an eleven year old kid. I know God heard me and sent His angel to answer my call."

The next time you are in the deep end of a swimming pool, try getting under someone and lifting him out of the water—without touching the sides or bottom of the pool. It is next to impossible. Trained lifeguards would have difficulty doing what was done that day, but his secret was *calling on God.* And, God was big enough to lift them both out of the pool.

We need to teach our children to call on God at a young age. Sometimes, however, our children can teach us a thing or two as you can see in this next story about our son.

Jack and Bill—not knowing there was an old underground gas well at the back of our 300 acre property—were burning brush. As you can imagine, when the fire got over the gas well it literally exploded, sending fire in every direction and igniting a nearby, tall, dry, grass field. Immediately, the fire was completely out of control. With no water lines back there at the time, they were fighting to no avail. The barrel of water they had in the back of the pickup didn't even make a dent in the flames.

Seeing that the fire was getting dangerously close to other fields that fed right in to the surrounding homes, Jack flew up to the house to call the fire department, sent me to meet them at the cross roads so they wouldn't get lost, and then dashed back—only to find that the fire was out. And, Bill, looking like he had been working in the coal mines, was sitting on a tree stump trying to catch his breath. Jack said, *"How on earth were you able to put out the fire—there was no way."* Bill's next words—*"I called on God"*—said it all.

You, too, can be delivered from *destruction.* For those out-of-control days, God is always there.

Chapter 18

...I will be with him in trouble; *I will rescue him...*
                                                                    –Psalm 91:15

T HE FOURTH PROMISE—TO *rescue from trouble* those who love the Lord—is found in the middle of verse 15. It is a well-known fact that human nature cries out to God when faced with trouble. Men in prison, soldiers in war, people in accidents… all seem to call out to God when they get in a crisis. Even atheists are known to call on *the God they don't acknowledge* when they are extremely afraid. A lot of criticism has been given to those kinds of *court of the last resort* prayers. However, in defense of this kind of praying, we must remember that when one is in pain, he usually runs to the one he loves the most and the one he trusts. The alternative is not calling out at all, so this verse acknowledges that calling out to God when we are in trouble is a good place to start.

If a person has never felt danger, he never thinks about needing protection. It is the one that knows he is in imminent danger who will appreciate and take the words of this psalm to heart. God has a great deal of variety in His plentiful means of protection and modes of rescue from trouble.

This verse also reminds me of a story that I read about a U.S. Senator during the pre-Civil War days, a story that is said to be true. The Senator had taken his son to the slave market where the boy noticed a black mother crying and praying as they were preparing to sell her daughter on the slave block. As he walked closer, he overheard the mother crying out, "*Oh, God, if I could help You as easily as You could help me, I'd do it for You, Lord.*" The young man was so touched by the prayer that he went over and bought the girl off the slave block and gave her back to her mother.

God answers our prayers and rescues us in so many different ways. I am so thankful that He is creative and not limited by our seemingly impossible situations. But, we have to ask in faith and not confine Him to our limited resources. God says, *"If you love Me, I will be with you when you find yourself in trouble, and I will rescue you."* But we have to trust Him to do it *His* way.

When you pass through the waters, I will be with you; and through the rivers, they will not overflow you. When you walk through the fire, you will not be scorched, nor will the flame burn you.
                                                    –Isaiah 43:2

I read a story several years ago about a woman who had a son in a war zone in World War II, and she wrote out Psalm 91 and sent it to him—explaining that those promises in Psalm 91 would be his protection. The son took it to his commanding officer who assigned his whole outfit to read the entire psalm out loud together every morning. She said that when the war was over—this was the only outfit she knew of in the war zone that reportedly had not one casualty.

Our son, Bill saw the *rescuing* power of God when he found himself in serious *trouble* after attempting to swim across a lake that was much wider than he calculated. With no strength left in his body and having already gone under twice, Bill experienced all the sensations of drowning. But miraculously, God not only provided a woman on the opposite bank, which was previously deserted, but also enabled her to throw a life ring (that just *happened* to be nearby) over 30 yards, landing within inches of his almost lifeless body. That was certainly Bill's *day of trouble*, but I thank God that He was with Bill, and *rescued* him.

Although some people might call happenings like these a coincidence, the negative situations that we encounter can become *God-incidences* when we trust His Word.

Chapter 19

God Honors Me

...I will *honor* him. —Psalm 91:15

THE FIFTH PROMISE—TO *honor* those who love God— is in the last part of verse fifteen. All of us like to be honored. I can remember the teacher calling my name when I was in grade school and complimenting a paper I had turned in. That thrilled me. I was honored.

It is truly a mind boggling concept to think the God of the universe would honor a person. Like the life of Joseph (Genesis 37-50), a person who has God's honor really stands out. *What does it look like when God places His honor on someone's life?*

While we were praying about this chapter, my daughter Angie, and I were discussing ways in which God honors someone. In the *Psalm 91 for Mothers* book, I recalled a humorous story on the reverse concept of honor, but in this chapter I wanted to give you an idea of what it means to be honored.

First of all, honor is sometimes hard to give, but we certainly like receiving it. A book could be written on what a powerful spiritual tool it is to give honor. However, let's start at this level, where God honors us. I can recall countless memories of how many times God has honored me, in spite of myself. It is a fabulous promise about honor in Psalm 91. When I think of honor, I always remember this story of a time when Angie was in elementary school...

Angie was taking art lessons once a week from an older couple whose studio was located downtown, and it was my job to pick her up. The lesson was over in the late afternoon, right at a very busy time of day. It came just as I was finishing up my day's work and trying to get dinner on the table before Jack got home from his weekly deacon's meeting. Invariably, I would lose track of the time and be a little late picking her up. It had not seemed to cause too much of a problem because the students were still putting away art supplies and tidying up as I arrived, but one night I was especially late getting to the studio. Angie was sitting on the curb while the art teacher and his wife sat in their car waiting for *this delinquent mom* to show up. I was so embarrassed that I made a private vow never to let that happen again. The next week I even put a reminder on my kitchen stove. However, about thirty minutes before time to leave to pick Angie up, an out of town friend knocked on my door. I was so excited to see her that we got involved instantly in a long, catch-up conversation, and I completely forgot about the time. When I suddenly thought of Angie, it was way past the time the class had ended, and I literally went into a panic. I was very late and I knew they would be waiting. I already had the mental, horror picture of them sitting in their car with Angie, humiliated, sitting on the curb. Same picture as the week before but only worse this time because I had done it again. The frantic explanation running through my mind sounded so feeble.

I was beside myself when I heard the still, small voice of the Lord say, "Can you trust Me to make you an overcomer even in spite of your mistake?" One of the hardest things I have ever done was to pull myself at that moment to a place of choosing to trust God and say, "*OK, Lord, I choose to believe you will honor me if I will trust You.*" Just as I made that declaration, I arrived at the art studio and the scene I saw through the picture window almost caused my heart to stop. Jack, who had never before picked Angie up from her art lessons in her life, was sitting in the art gallery talking and laughing with the art teacher. By this time it was almost an hour past closing time, but Jack had gotten there in time and they were just enjoying a leisurely visit. They never even knew I had been late. Jack had been on time, yet how did he know, since he had never picked her up before.

Later, still in a state of shock, I asked Jack why he happened to decide to pick her up that night. He simply said, "The deacon's meeting was called off." I had so many questions, I just began firing them off—"*You've never picked her up before so why this time? How did you know what time she was through? What made you even remember that she took art lessons on Wednesday night since we are always home by the time your deacon's meeting is over?*" He just looked puzzled and said, "I don't know."

But, I knew! I just stood there in a state of shock thinking of how God had honored me in spite of myself. It was overwhelming to realize the honor God can bestow when I chose to trust Him.

God is so faithful to fulfill His promises if we look to Him in faith. I felt like old Abraham when God chose to honor him before Abimelech, even though Abraham had certainly done nothing to deserve it (Genesis 20). This lets me know that when a person is honored by God, it has very little to do with the person. Honor is a gift God gives us. Because we love Him, He honors us.

Chapter 20

God Satisfies Me With Long Life

With a long life I will satisfy him. —Psalm 91:16a

T HE SIXTH PROMISE—TO *satisfy* those who love Him with *a long life*—is found in verse 16. God does not just say that He will prolong our lives and give us a lot of birthdays. No! He says that He will *satisfy* us with a long life. There are people who would testify that just having a great many birthdays is not necessarily a blessing. But, God says that He will give us many birthdays, and as those birthdays roll around we will experience satisfaction.

It has been said that there is a *God shaped vacuum* on the inside of each one of us. Man has tried to fill that vacuum with many different things, but nothing will satisfy that emptiness until it is filled with Jesus. That is the true satisfaction to which God refers in His Promise. God is making the offer. If we will come to Him, let Him fill that empty place on the inside and allow Him to fulfill the call on our lives—then He will give us *a long life* and *satisfy* us as we live it out. Only the dissatisfied person can really appreciate what it means to find satisfaction.

It is a fact that God wants us to live a satisfied life, but let's also not neglect the promise of a long life. King David was Israel's most valiant, daring warrior, yet he lived to be a ripe old age—*"full of days"* as the Old Testament authors liked to say. His life was filled with combat, high risk situations, and impossible odds. Yet, he did not die in battle; his head went down in peace in his old age. Long life is a great concluding promise of protection.

Paul lets us know in Ephesians, however, that we are in a fight. We can't flow with the wide road—with what feels good, and still win this battle because the enemy will make the wrong path extremely easy to take. Eddie Rickenbacker, the World War I flying ace, who had near-death experiences throughout his life, once wanted to let himself die, but later said this about death—*"I felt the presence of death, and I knew that I was going.* **You may have heard that dying is unpleasant, but don't you believe it.** *Dying is the* **sweetest, tenderest, most sensuous** *sensation I have ever experienced.* **Death comes disguised** *as a sympathetic friend. All was serene; all was calm. How wonderful it would be simply to float out of this world.* **It is easy to die.** *You have to* **fight to live.** *And, that is what I did. I recognized that wonderful,* **mellow sensation** *for what it was—death—and I fought it. I literally* **fought death in my mind,** *pushing away the sweet blandishments and* **welcoming back the pain.** *The next ten days were a continuous fight with the old Grim Reaper, and,* *again and again, I would feel myself start to slip away. Each time I rallied and fought back, until I had turned the corner toward recovery.*" Captain Rickenbacker should know! Death came toward him many times during his service as a soldier in both world wars: when he survived two plane crashes and when he was lost for twenty-four days in the Pacific Ocean.

Sometimes the spirit of death makes a bid for our very life. It is these inner dynamics that are at work when a person is wounded, facing a serious illness, wracked by pain from an injury or sensing impending doom. It is easy to give in to it. We think of the ugly side to destruction, but the danger is when it comes with a pretty face. It is a fight to break free from the enticing call of death, persevere to victory and receive this covenant promise of a *satisfied, long life.*

Once, in a boat on the Sea of Galilee, the disciples cried out in fear that they would drown in the storm. Jesus, however, had said that they must go to the other side. If they had thought through what He'd said, they would have known that the storm would not harm them because they had His word on a mission across the lake. In the same way, if you have been promised a satisfied, long life, then you know you will make it through the present circumstances.

God wants us to claim the promise of long life, but He also wants us to use that long life for Him. Ask yourself, "What *am* I going to do with my long life?"

Chapter 21

Behold His Salvation

...and let him behold My Salvation.   –Psalm 91:16b

ALLOWING THOSE WHO LOVE Him to *behold His salvation* is the seventh promise found in the last part of verse 16. *Behold* simply means to see something and *take hold of it and make it our own.* God wants us to take hold of His salvation.

The movement of this last line in Psalm 91 describes our ultimate, final victory. The order of this sentence gives us promise that we will see salvation face to face DURING AND AFTER our *long, satisfied life.* This moves us beyond an intellectual knowledge of salvation to relationship. It secures our future, but it starts now. Jesus constantly reminded us that, "Salvation is Now! Today it has come!" Many people are surprised when they look up the word "salvation" in a Bible concordance and find that it has a much deeper meaning than just *a ticket to heaven.* We often miss the richness of this promise.

According to *Strong's Exhaustive Concordance,* the Word translated *salvation* includes health, healing, deliverance, rescue, safety, protection and provision. What more could we ask? God promises that He will allow us to see and *take hold of* His Life, His Health, His Healing, His Deliverance, His Protection and His Provision!

Many people read Psalm 91 and simply see it with their eyes, but very few *behold* it in their lives. My prayer is for that to change. One of my biggest thrills, after teaching this truth of God, is having different people write or call, describing the ecstatic joy of having it come alive in their heart. I love to hear the extent to which they have actually taken hold of this covenant and started experiencing it as a vital part of their existence.

In the testimonies that follow, your heart will be encouraged by those who have beheld first-hand the salvation of the Lord. Read their stories in their own words. The truth about God's salvation—His protection, deliverance, health and provision—is more than just wishful thinking. It is a promise of which one can actually take hold.

SUMMARY

Nothing in this world can be relied upon as confidently as God's promises, when we believe them, refuse to waver and decide to make His Word *our final authority* for every area of life...

I believe that Psalm 91 is a covenant (a spiritual contract) that God has made available to His children—especially in these difficult days. But, there are some who sincerely ask, *"How do you know that you can take a **song** from the psalms and base your life on it?"* Jesus answered that question. The value of the psalms was emphasized when He cited them as a source of Truth that must be fulfilled.

> *Now He said to them, "These are My words which I spoke to you while I was still with you, that all things which are written about Me in the law of Moses and the Prophets AND THE PSALMS must be fulfilled (emphasis added)."*
>
> –Luke 24:44

When Jesus specifically equated the psalms to the Law of Moses and the Prophets, we see that it is historically relevant, prophetically sound and totally applicable and reliable.

At a time when there are so many uncertainties facing us, it is more than comforting to know that God not only knows ahead of time what we will be facing, but He also made absolute provision for us.

Someone once pointed out, *"It is interesting that the world must have gotten its distress 911 number from God's answer to our distress call —Psalm "91-1."*

It seems only a dream now to think back on the time when my mind was reeling in fears and doubts. Little did I know when I asked God that pertinent question —*"Is there any way for a Christian to escape all the evils that are coming on this world?"*—He was going to give me a dream that would not only change my life, but also change the lives of thousands of others who would hear and believe.

Our minds cannot even begin to comprehend God's goodness. **TRULY, WHAT A MIGHTY GOD WE SERVE.**

What Must I Do To Be Saved?

We've talked about physical protection. Now let's make sure that you have eternal protection. The promises from God in this book are for God's children who love Him. If you have never given your life to Jesus and accepted Him as your Lord and Savior, there is no better time than right now.

There is none righteous, not even one.
—Romans 3:10

...for all have sinned and fallen short of the glory of God. —Romans 3:23

God loves you and gave His life that you might live eternally with Him.

But God demonstrates His own love toward us, in that while we were yet sinners, Christ died for us.
—Romans 5:8

For God so loved the world (you), that He gave His only begotten Son, that whoever believes in Him should not perish but have eternal life.
—John 3:16

There is nothing we can do to earn our salvation or to make ourselves good enough to go to heaven. It is a free gift!

The wages of sin is death, but the free gift of God is eternal life in Christ Jesus.   –Romans 6:23

There is also no other avenue through which we can reach heaven, other than Jesus Christ—God's Son.

And there is salvation in no one else; for there is no other name under heaven that has been given among men, by which we must be saved.
   –Acts 4:12

Jesus said to him, "I am the Way, and the Truth, and the Life; no one comes to the Father, but through Me."   –John 14:6

You must believe that Jesus is the Son of God, that He died on the cross for your sins, and that He rose again on the third day.

...who (Jesus) was declared with power to be the Son of God by the resurrection from the dead...
   –Romans 1:4

You may be thinking, "How do I accept Jesus and become His child?" God in His Love has made it so easy.

If you confess with your mouth the Lord Jesus and believe in your heart that God raised Him from the dead, you shall be saved.
   –Romans 10:9

But as many as received Him, to them He gave the right to become children of God, even to those who believe in His Name.   –John 1:12

It is as simple as praying a prayer similar to this one—if you sincerely mean it in your heart:

Dear God:

I believe You gave your Son, Jesus, to die for me. I believe He shed His Blood to pay for my sins and that You raised Him from the dead so I can be Your child and live with You eternally in heaven. I am asking Jesus to come into my heart right now and save me. I confess You as the Lord and Master of my life.

I thank You, dear Lord, for loving me enough to lay down your life for me. Take my life now and use it for Your Glory. I ask for all that You have for me.

In Jesus Name,
Amen

Jennifer McCullough
Howard Payne University
Southwestern Baptist Theological Seminary

Murders in the Village

Before leaving for East Africa in 1999, I was being discipled by Angelia Schum, my college Bible study teacher. It was a crash course in *everything you need to know before entering "the Bush!"* I ran into her friend Donna one night at church. She said, *"You do know about Psalm 91, don't you?"* When I said, *"No!"*—she said, *"Angie must not love you very much if she hasn't told you about Psalm 91!"*

I began intently studying the chapter and memorized it before I left. I had no idea the power this passage has until January

15th, 2000. I lived in a village in the bush with the Ankole tribe (cattle herders), working with orphans with AIDS and teaching at the village school. I often found myself praying Psalm 91 while walking the circumference of the village. I had gone to the city the day before on the milk truck. That night I was lying in my hut and heard gunshots. I ran to a fellow missionary's hut and sat in a small room praying Psalm 91 over and over. The husband was out investigating, so it was just a 24 year old mother, her two year old child and me.

In the meantime, a group of rebels were raiding our village. Men were shot, a pregnant woman was beaten, villagers were robbed and cattle were stolen. The villagers were laid out in a line on their stomachs with guns and machetes pointed to their heads, while they were being threatened not to say a word. The raid was well planned as they had been watching us for days from the bushes.

Here is the miracle! Village people know that white missionaries have more in their huts than Ugandans make in a lifetime. Yet, the rebels never came to our hut—in spite of the fact that everyone else's hut was raided. After the fact, the rebels admitted to the police that they had followed the milk truck through the bush the night before the raid. I had been on that truck sitting next to the driver who was carrying two million shillings—the villagers' monthly income from the milk sales. They did not attack the truck in route because we had returned before dark that night. This was the first time we had ever returned before dark in the six months I had been riding the route.

The day after the attack it was very intense. I walked through the village, praying for villagers who had been robbed and beaten. They had looks of pure terror on their faces, knowing that the rebels were still hiding in the bush nearby. While talking to the villagers, no one could believe that I was not attacked. My interpreter, Segambe, said, *"It was as if your hut was not even there."*

God is faithful! He has a perfect plan for your life! God is all knowing! He will give you weapons to fight the battles you face.

God did not give Psalm 91 only to missionaries in the African bush. He gave it to everyone so that we can daily claim His promises to us as Christians. I find the words of Psalm 91 in my daily prayers: *"...He will cover me with His feathers, and under His wings I find refuge. His faithfulness is my shield and rampart..."*

Don't miss the chance to see the power of God's promises in your life. Claim them, memorize them, pray them, and live them. He is faithful!

02.08.2007 17:29

Dane Kaley
Miracle told by Vicki Jackson

Author's Note: *Our good friends, Vicki and Gerald Jackson, live in Fort Worth, Texas. Vicki called to tell me this amazing story that happened to one of their fellow church members, Dane Kaley.*

Dane Kaley developed a small growth in his ear in January. The doctor decided to remove it in day surgery, however, the *minor* surgery turned out not to be so minor. A biopsy revealed the growth to be squamous carcinomas, a very dangerous and aggressive form of skin cancer. He was told to go immediately to an oncologist. Vicki began spending two to three hours every day encouraging Dane and his wife, Diana, with God's covenant promise in Psalm 91. The prognosis from the oncologist/surgeon was grim and frightening. Dane was then sent for a PET scan that showed the cancer had metastasized into the bones in front of and behind his ear. It had also spread to the lymph nodes on the left side of his neck and surgery was immediately scheduled. Two CAT scans were done the day before the surgery. Vicki said she had never interceded so much for one person before Dane. The Lord even woke her in the middle of the night to pray, and He gave her a vision of how He was going to use Dane to touch his church and usher in a fresh outpouring of the Holy Spirit.

On the day of the surgery Vicki and Diana were permitted to go into a restricted area to pray for Dane, and as they prayed everything came to a complete stop. Even the doctors joined them in prayer. Then, three hours later one of the doctors came out to share THE GOOD NEWS! They had begun the surgery by removing the cancerous growth along with surrounding tissue. The tissue was sent to pathology to make sure they had reached the outer parameters of the unhealthy cells. They also made an incision down the left side of Dane's neck to prepare to remove the lymph nodes along with "all other glands" to insure the disease would be contained.

Can you imagine the surprise of the doctors when the report came back from pathology and the test showed the very dangerous and aggressive skin cancer wasn't squamous at all, but basal cell carcinomas—which very rarely spread to any other part of the body! The doctors closed Dane's neck and did not remove the lymph nodes.

In addition, the doctor told them that the CAT scans prior to surgery had shown a completely different story from the PET scan the week prior. The first CAT scan indicated there was no cancer in the nodes, so the second scan was done—this one indicating there was no cancer in the nodes or bone! The disease was retreating before their very eyes and by the time they did the surgery, the threat of death had been rebuked by the Lord.

The doctor was confused and kept saying, "I don't know how this happened!" It was all Vicki and Diana could do to keep from just running and praising through the hospital. Dane was supposed to be in the hospital for several days and then have chemo and radiation treatment, but he went home the day after surgery, cancer free. Thank God, *"the things which are seen are temporal and subject to change...,"* according to 2 Corinthians 4:18.

Hayley Platt

I have read the Psalm 91 book so many times and I love it. There are different lessons for different seasons, but Psalm 91 is for every season. I still pray it out loud every morning. The part that stands out is the fact that angels are there escorting us though our every day, bearing us up in their hands in order that we not even stumble. God is so committed to escorting us that He furnished us with bodyguards. He certainly sent angels to escort me through my time of taking chemo and birthing a baby in the middle of those treatments.

The drug I was being given was bright red. For some reason, I think because of the color, it was very scary watching it come down the IV tube and enter my veins. As the bright red liquid got closer and closer to my arm, I started to panic. I remember that I began demanding to have my Bible. I heard myself saying, "Where is my Bible! Where is my Bible?" I got so panicked that even the nurse became frightened and started saying, "Someone, get her a Bible." My husband, Jonathan, and the nurse were digging through my things desperately trying to locate one. When they finally found it, I started thumbing through the pages until I got to Psalm 91 and began reading it as fast as I could. I was watching the IV and looking at my Bible and just as the red liquid reached my arm, I finished reading the passage. Instantly, my peace came back and I began saying, "I can ...drink any deadly poison and it will not harm me..." [Mark 16:17-18]. Chemo is a poison, intended to eradicate the cancer, but it can also be deadly to other parts of the body. However, God had promised me in His word that this deadly poison would not be able to harm me. It could only harm the cancer. Normally, all of this procedure takes place while one is under anesthesia, but they couldn't put me to sleep since I was pregnant. I had to be awake for every course of action and all they could give me was a local of Lidocaine. It didn't help that I could hear the doctors in the next room talking about what they ate for lunch. You feel desperate to have them focus on your situation, but I had to remember they do this all day. Nevertheless, to you, it is the most serious thing in the world at that moment.

The next procedure I had was the installation of the port placement so that I could receive chemo directly to the area. Thankfully, they allowed me to listen to whatever music I chose during the procedure. Sadly, that day the speakers were broken. The room is sterile and you're not allowed to bring anything in with you, but I kept telling the Lord, "I cannot do this without worship music." I was really scared because the tubing is threaded up and down close to your heart. I was nervous having anything put that close to such a vital organ. I am sure it was no big deal to the nurses and doctors, but it made me very apprehensive. I was still telling the Lord that I needed worship music when the nurse said, "If you want to take your phone in with you, sneak it under the pillow and you can listen to your worship music." I was so grateful. It was a totally sterile room, yet she let me bring my cell phone in. I had the volume turned down really low and I just lay there and listened in a supernatural cocoon of peace.

I had an MRI done, and the lady who did it was a believer and realized that I was panicked at what it might do to my baby. I was on my back with a board on top of me and they were getting ready to put me through a 'kid' tube since all the adult tubes were taken. It was a tiny little opening and I had a very big belly. With that thought, I started compulsively shaking, unable to control my body. It got so bad that the table I was lying on began shaking the machine. When the nurse saw what was happening, she just leaned over me and began saying over and over, "God is good! God is good! Breathe in! God is good! Breathe out! God is good!" That went on for an hour and twenty minutes, and I was fine. Then, I started singing to the Lord, "You are the famous One." I couldn't remember anything except that one song, so I just sang that over and over—"You are the famous One! The famous One!"

God had put a nurse with me who perfectly demonstrated God's kindness and His awesome peace. It was as though the Lord was touching me through her touch to bring me through the chemo miraculously.

Then, the birth! I could tell the doctors were highly concerned about the birth. The cancer had appeared during the 20th week of my pregnancy, so I had been receiving chemo treatments during the second half of my pregnancy, and now 20 weeks later, it was time for Gabriella to come into the world. They were worried I wouldn't have the strength to push her out. However, God is an awesome God and He gave me a supernatural delivery. My water broke and an hour and ten minutes later, my baby was born—pain free!

To add to the miracle, I had my baby with no medication. There was no time for medication. I had some slight discomfort with the contractions, but once it moved over to pushing contractions, I felt nothing. Even when I pushed Gabriella out, I felt nothing! (According to my friend Cathy, it was nothing short of a miracle because her description of giving birth was the worst thing she had ever experienced in her entire life. She said it felt as though her loins were being ripped out of her.) Even though I wanted medication, there was no time for it. Not long before the birth, I told the nurse that it might be time for the epidural. She made the call, then checked me and excitedly proclaimed, "Honey, you are a 'ten'. You went from a zero to a ten in ten minutes. I have never seen this happen before." Instantly, she then picked up the phone, and said, "Cancel the anesthesiologist and call the doctor. The baby is coming right now." Upon hearing the nurse's excitement, there was a moment when fear tried to grip me. I have heard people talk about liquid fear, and suddenly, I knew what liquid fear felt like. It was hot and I could feel it try to enter me, but during my quiet time the day before, God had spoken to me, "Perfect love will cast out all fear." Outloud I said, "Lord, You said that perfect love casts out all fear and You love me perfectly, therefore, I will not fear." I kept saying, "It is just

You and me, Jesus." The whole time I was saying that, the nurse was just typing and looking at the monitor. I wondered if she thought, "We've got a crazy one on our hands."

The moment I said, "Perfect love casts out fear because the Lord loves me perfectly, it went fine." All the fear was gone! For a moment, all I could hear in my head was Cathy telling me that it felt like her loins were being ripped out, so I had to get that voice out of my mind and, instead, begin concentrating on what God was saying. The doctor didn't even have time to wash his hands.   I heard the nurse say, "She's coming out. You need to turn around now!" And, instantly, she just slid out with no pain!!

I was told that because of the chemo, my baby would be underweight, but to everyone's surprise, my precious little "underweight" baby weighed 8 pounds and 10 ounces!

Another interesting thing happened when I went in to get the PET Scan. The PET Scan nurse, who had been in cancer remission for ten years, said, "How long have you been in remission and how many years ago did you stop doing chemo?" I responded, "Oh, I'm right in the middle of chemo now". She was shocked and just kept touching my arm, saying, "Oh my! Your skin is so beautiful. You look absolutely great!" She thought I had been through chemo years ago and I was just coming in for an annual PET Scan.

Before that, I hadn't realized that chemo almost always changes the skin color.

On one visit to the doctor, I asked, "Is this just a light chemo treatment?" She laughed and said, "First of all, all chemo is rigorous. No chemo is light. The plan we have you on is quite an intense form of chemo. And, I have to tell you that most of my patients lose their hair and most of them do not handle it well. She said that they do fairly well on the first treatment and some do well on the second treatment, but, from there it is always downhill." She told me that I was discussed every day in the conference room because I confused them. "We don't know why you are doing so well, but I have to say that you have baffled us." I found I was on a very strong chemo treatment. It is a common treatment, but strong. My blood count was also amazing—it was off the charts, even for a healthy person. And, especially, for a pregnant person, it was unexplainable.

What an awesome God we serve! I stand amazed at His miracles—no cancer now, baby birthed perfectly and painlessly, no hair loss, no funny coloring, and the chemo poisoning didn't harm me or my precious baby...God is indeed an amazing Father! I can do nothing but give God all the honor and glory during this period of my life because it has been a miracle every step of the way.

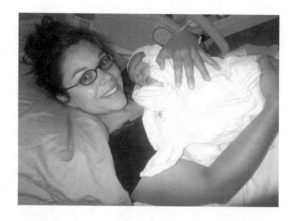

Hayley's dream 2 days before she went to the doctor...

In my dream, I was in Brownwood (Brownwood is where I lived while I was going to college at Howard Payne University) and my car broke down or I ran out of gas. I pulled over and got out of the car and started walking. I had no idea where I was supposed to go. This voice said, "Turn left here. Peggy Joyce [Ruth] lives down this street. You need to go down this street." I passed by the 3M company and the closer I got to their house the more I started to recognize where I was. All of a sudden Peggy Joyce [PJ] comes out on her front porch and points at me and says, "Come inside. Come inside." I told her my car had broken down and I didn't know where to go and this voice told me to come down this street and there you are.

So she said, "Come on in. We have been waiting on you." So I went inside and we were in the living room and a bunch of my family members are there. I went out in the back yard and there are two crocodiles—a large one and a small one. They were trying to get me and I ran back into the living room and then into the kitchen. The crocodiles were after me and I got up on the counter and PJ said, "Use your Scripture. Use your Scripture." Then, I said, "Psalm 91 is my Scripture." So I picked up a frying pan. Psalm 91 was the frying pan. I started beating the large crocodile and killed it with the frying pan. Then the small one started trying to get to me so I started beating it with the frying pan. I kept saying Psalm 91 but I couldn't kill it so I put the frying pan down. Then PJ said, "Your Father has it taken care of." You beat it but it is still alive but Your Father will sever its head. It will be ok. Your Father will take care of it."

Then I went to the doctor. I didn't know at the time that I had two tumors: a large one and a small one. It was a couple of days after the dream that I found out about the two tumors. The large tumor was easy to get rid of but the small one was not as easy to kill. They are both dead now and taken care of. The cancer is gone but when I found out that I had the two tumors I had peace. I knew I had my Psalm 91 Scripture and that it was going to be beaten so it wasn't as shocking or fearful when the doctor delivered the news. I felt prepared in my spirit for it. I used my Psalm 91 Scripture and it worked.

When the doctor told me about the two tumors, I thought—"Those are my two crocodiles." It was kind of funny that I was hitting them with a frying pan. But I knew in my dream that the frying pan was my Scripture. Like I said, "They are both dead now and taken care of. The cancer is gone, but God was so good to give me the answer before I even knew I would fight cancer."

Alma Reyes

God's Psalm 91 Covenant of Protection works for anyone, at any time, under any circumstances if we run to God and determine to declare His protection promises in faith. But, too often fear or the world's influence causes us to waver in our faith and miss our miracle. However, that was not the case with Alma Reyes! While we were in Bacolod City in the Philippines we found out about this remarkable testimony that had taken place right in the area where we were ministering. Bacolod is a large city, bustling with activity while jeepney mini-buses and bicycle carts carry people to their destinations.

On one particular day, less than a year after Alma had accepted Jesus as her Lord and Savior, she got a chance to prove the faithfulness of her God. As usual, she was in a jeepney on her way to work. It was routine for the van to stop many times along the way, picking up other passengers until the driver had a full load, but this particular morning Alma had such an uneasiness that she began to pray silently. When the van reached a more secluded area two men suddenly commanded the driver to stop, stepped off the van, drew out a gun and pointed it to the man sitting next to Alma. Perhaps, it was the scripture, "I will not die but live and proclaim what the Lord has done for me," that God had given to Alma just a month after she got saved that gave her so much confidence that she felt no fear. But, when the gunman fired his gun, hitting the man sitting next to Alma in the shoulder, she was the only one on the van who didn't begin screaming hysterically. The panic was so great that an old Chinese man began having a heart attack just as the gunman put his gun to the already wounded man's head, shot and killed him instantly. That was too much. Instead of cringing in fear, a confident boldness in God's protection rose up on the inside of Alma and she turned to look straight into the eyes of the killer, making him so intimidated that he turned his gun to point it directly between Alma's eyes. But, before he was able to pull the trigger, she was taking her authority in the Name of Jesus, commanding Satan, in Jesus' Name, to loose His hold on the man. It was obvious that the man was trying to pull the trigger, but his hand was paralyzed and he couldn't move his finger. He tried three times to shoot Alma, to no avail. The driver finally took off, leaving the killer standing in the road with his gun raised and still trying to shoot it, but it was not until they were out of the killer's range that they heard his gun fire.

By this time everyone's attention was directed toward the old man who was having the heart attack. Alma called to the driver to take the man to the hospital, but as they were going she took his hand and began praying. At that moment the power of God surged through her and he was instantly healed. He was so well that by the time they reached the hospital the old man wouldn't let them take him in because he said that there was no need since he was completely well.

Psalm 91 speaks of the authority that we have been given over the powers of darkness when we decide to use it. Alma is a living testimony to that truth.

Audra _Chasteen_

gave in her own words this testimony—
of her son, Skylar

About 7:30 in the evening on July 28, 2001, three of my sisters and I, along with our children, were visiting my parents. Skylar, my four year old, was riding bicycles with the older boys out in the pasture about a half mile from the house. I had just turned to warn my older son not to ride down the hill because of the steep incline, when I realized that Skylar had already started down. The next thing I

knew the bicycle was out of control and he had gone over the side of a cliff. When I got to him he wasn't moving and he wasn't crying. He was tangled in the wheel of the bicycle, lying on his stomach with his chin twisted past his shoulder, resting on his shoulder blade. It was a terrifying sight to see Skylar's head bent almost backwards. His left arm was back behind him with his wrist above his right shoulder. His eyes were half open, in a fixed position, down and to the corner. He was blue and not breathing.

When I saw Skylar in that distorted position and not breathing, I didn't have to be told that it was bad. I just started screaming. In spite of the obvious head and neck injury, I turned his head forward so that he could breathe. But, when he still didn't start breathing—I turned his whole body straight, hoping that would help. When that didn't work, I became hysterical. My three sisters and I are nurses, one RN and three LVN, but we couldn't seem to pull ourselves together to know what to do medically. It was as though none of us had one brain cell functioning. My sister Donna just picked him up and stood there.

When my oldest sister, Cynthia, finally got to the scene of the accident, the first thing she did was to lay her hand over on Skylar's head and start rebuking the enemy. She kept saying, "I rebuke you, Satan, in the Name of Jesus—you get your hands off Skylar—you cannot have him!" Then she started pleading the Blood of Jesus and quoting Psalm 91 over him. Hearing God's Word coming out of Cynthia's mouth pulled me back to my senses. I sent one of my sisters for her car, and we headed for the nearest hospital—which was about seventeen miles away.

On the way to the hospital we did some rescue breaths on Skylar, and he would breathe for a few minutes and then stop. I tried to hold his head and neck straight, but the whole time his eyes were still fixed. Cynthia and I continued to speak Psalm 91 over Skylar and to command his body to line up with God's Word—but nothing was coming out as eloquently as I wanted. All that I could say was, "Bones, be like you're supposed to be—Body, be like you are supposed to be—in Jesus' Name."

I remember thinking—"God, how can you ask us to praise You in *every* situation—how can I praise you when my child is in danger?" And I felt like the Lord impressed me, "Just do it—you don't have to know why—just do it!" I was able to give God one sentence—"Lord, I give you the Glory and the Honor and the Praise." (I wasn't giving God the praise from thinking that He sent this situation—I was giving God the praise because of *who He is* and because His Word said to praise Him in all things.) The whole way we prayed in the Spirit and quoted Psalm 91 over him.

When we got to the hospital in Comanche, Texas, they immediately put a neck brace on him, but he still wasn't responding. By then he had started breathing on his own, but his eyes were still fixed. Then he started throwing up—another sign of a bad head injury.

As soon as they had Skylar in X-ray, I called one of our pastors to get some of the intercessors praying. I knew we needed help. As much as we had been taught, I was still unprepared when the tragedy actually happened. As he prayed, peace came over me and I suddenly knew that everything was going to be OK.

The X-rays showed an obvious break in the C-1 vertebra (the first vertebra under the head) and Skylar still wasn't responding. He was immediately, with the X-rays, air-flighted to Cook's Children's Hospital in Fort Worth, TX.

Since I was still in my scrubs from working all day, they didn't realize at Cook's Hospital that I was the mother, so they had me helping to draw the blood on Skylar. I was listening as the trauma nurse reported to the doctor when he came in –"he has a C-1 fracture, his eyes are deviated and down to the left, he stopped breathing, etc." The doctor was shocked when he discovered I was the mother. I could never have been that peaceful without all the prayers.

The only thing that seemed to calm Skylar while we were waiting was to put my hand on his forehead and pray Psalm 91 over him. Even though Skylar was not awake through all of this, once when I paused in my praying, Skylar said, "Amen!" From the moment that he responded from an unconscious state— giving his agreement to that prayer—I knew he would be fine, in spite of the seriousness of his condition. Finally, they wheeled him in for more X-rays and for a CAT scan to see if there was any bleeding in the brain cavity.

When the doctor finally came in he had a very strange look on his face, and all he could say was, "He's going to be all right!" Then, after consulting with the radiologist, they came in saying, **"We don't know how to explain this, but we can find no head trauma (brain swelling or bleeding) and we cannot find a C-1 fracture."** They had the Comanche hospital X-rays with the obvious break, but their X-rays showed no sign of a break.

There are no words to describe the joy and the gratitude and the excitement that we felt at that moment. All the nurses were pouring in to tell us how *lucky* we were and all I could say was, "Luck had nothing to do with this. This was God!" I was not about to let Satan have one ounce of glory. I knew that it was a miracle and that it was God who had healed him, however, he still wasn't responding very well so they put us in the pediatric ward of the ICU to monitor him. The next morning the nurse came in and scratched him on the head, assuming she would get the same response (nothing) that she had gotten the day before.

But this time when she scratched him and called out his name he said, "What?" Everyone, including the nurse, jumped – and then rejoiced!

From that point on he was able to wake up and respond. The doctor was just amazed. He said, "I don't know what to tell you. There was definitely a break on that other X-ray, but he is obviously OK now. I don't know how to explain it." He didn't have to explain it. I knew what had happened. God is so good!

Skylar has always been very close to my mother, and I found out something very interesting after we got home. Two weeks prior to the accident, Skylar had been telling her that it was time for him to go be with Jesus. And, mother would say, "No, Skylar, why would you say that? It's not time for you to go be with Jesus." But he would emphatically say, "Yes, it is! I've got to go" And she would argue with him, but she said she didn't think too much about it since he's only four years old. But, after the accident my mother knew that there was warfare going on, and it was God's promise in Psalm 91 that finally won the battle.

Since the day we left the hospital, Skylar has been a perfectly normal, healthy little boy with no problems and no side effects from the accident. He is truly a miracle!

Rene Hood

I will begin my testimony in July, 1998. At this point in my life I had eaten almost nothing for approximately two months—yet I continued to gain weight. I could not go outside in the direct sunlight for any length of time without my face becoming irritated to the point that if you placed your hand on my face the print of your hand would remain there. I had also begun to develop black spots on my face, arms and legs. Later, a red rash appeared throughout my body. Bruises would appear without my falling or having been hit.

During the month of July, my energy level was so low that it was a challenge to just clean the bathtub after bathing. My body became racked with pain—even when trying to perform a task as simple as brushing my teeth. One particular night is still fresh in my memory. For the past week or so, I had been choking when I would lie down at night. This night was the same but when I got up that morning I made the shocking discovery that I couldn't perform normal bodily functions. Knowing that something had to be done quickly, I called my doctor early that morning. After his examination he referred me to Scott and White Hospital to see Dr. Nichols, a nephrologist.

The night prior to my seeing Dr. Nichols my body aches had reached a new level and it had become a norm for me to have a fever of 103 or more. I felt like my brain was frying and I would lie on my bathroom floor in misery. My brown body transformed before my eyes into a gray color, covered with perspiration and rolled up in a fetal position. I told the Lord that it would be so easy to give up the ghost and just go home to be with Him, but I said, "Lord, I know that You are not finished with me. Lord, I hurt so badly and yet I know that there are people out there that You have called me to touch. My kids need me! I know I am walking in the *valley of the shadow of death, but I will fear no evil.* You promised me, Lord, in Psalm 91 that *only with my eyes would I see the reward of the wicked—that a thousand would fall at my side and ten thousand at my right hand, but it would not come nigh me.*"

My 18 year old daughter was home for the summer at the time and since my husband wasn't concerned, and told me so, she took me to Temple hospital. I was so weak that I could barely walk. After about a 25 minute examination the nephrologist, with no bedside manner and no sense of caring, said, "I give you three months and you will just go 'poop'." I was very angry that he would speak such words to me in the presence of my daughter, without any sensitivity. Then he said, "It will not be easy because you will be in a lot of pain, but (as he pointed to my daughter) she's big enough—she can take care of herself." Then he walked out the door. I looked at my daughter and assured her, "Mom is not going anywhere."

I was hospitalized, running a high fever and unable to eat. I would have involuntary shakes that I couldn't control and my right lung had collapsed because of the mass of protein my kidneys were now throwing into my system. I looked like a seven month pregnant woman. My kidneys were shutting down, my joints ached and were swollen, and the doctors had found a mass on my liver. After twelve days of their making one mistake after another and causing me more suffering without my getting any better, I asked my daughter to help me dress and take me back home to Bangs because God was going to give me a miracle.

I am a living testimony of His faithfulness to His promises. I went to my parent's house and I would sit up and walk as well as I could—reminding God of what He had promised—*"You will not be afraid of the deadly pestilence. It will not approach you."*

My local doctor would call and remind me that those specialists said I was dying and that I needed to be in a hospital. I wouldn't! I couldn't! I knew that *"greater is He that is in me than he that is in the world."* I had a supernatural peace that I was well and that the healing would manifest itself soon—so I kept pressing.

Since I would not go back to the hospital and my condition, by sight, was no better, my doctor encouraged me to go to a nephrologist in Abilene, TX. I finally agreed but refused the medicine because of the side effects. Not one doctor gave me one ounce of hope, but I was determined to receive the healing that Christ had provided. Then, the miracle started manifesting. It was during that next few months that I gradually started feeling better and my strength started returning. Finally, after seeing the Abilene doctor for two months and once again being put through a battery of tests, he stated, "I'm looking at your paperwork and I'm looking at you. If you had let us do what we wanted to do—and you wouldn't—we doctors would be patting ourselves on the back, saying we had gotten you in remission. All I can say is—whatever you have been doing, just keep doing it." Then he told me that I was a "miracle."

My doctor had a liver Specialist meet me at the Brownwood hospital and after a CAT scan and two sonograms, he could not find any mass in my liver. I was then sent to a blood Specialist, and after reading the reports he repeated twice that I was "a wonder." I have seen ten Christmases since being told that I would not live to see another Christmas.

My prison ministry didn't suffer and souls continue to be saved, delivered and set free because I abided in God's Word and trusted Him to be faithful. I have a book out called *Being Found in His Word*. We all need to be in His Word—refusing, no matter what—to be driven from His promises. I know that this battle and subsequent victory give honor to a "faithful, loving, and caring God" who desires to be embraced by each one of us.

Actor James Stewart
Air Force Combat Pilot
and Bombardier Trainer
Brigadier General, USAF

Christmas Eve, 1943, found Jimmy Stewart's bed empty. A cot on a drafty concrete floor, in a cold Nissen hut in Tibenham, northeast of London was a far cry from growing up in Indiana, Pennsylvania, surrounded by a warm and loving family and definitely a world away from his life before the war. After earning a degree in architecture at Princeton, he'd made a career move to Hollywood and earned an Oscar in 1940, for his role in *The Philadelphia Story*. Prior to that, he'd been nominated for Best Actor in 1939, for *Mr. Smith Goes to Washington.*

No one needed to remind him that Tibenham wasn't a Hollywood set, although he could have played the staring role in *Mr. Stewart Goes to War* if such a movie existed.

Jimmy joined the US Air Force in 1941, even before the emotional Pearl Harbor attack made most men angry enough to sign up. Nine months prior to the attack on Pearl Harbor, Jimmy had realized that war was inevitable. At 32, and already a pilot himself, he'd been the first Hollywood star to enlist for World War II. Refusing to spend his military career entertaining troops or making training films, he'd already worked his way up from private to captain in the 445th Bomb Group, flying missions deep into the heart of Nazi Germany.

First trained to pilot the B-17 Flying Fortress, Jimmy now flew the bigger, faster and newer B-24 Bomber. Fully loaded, it carried a crew of ten. Each of the four moveable turrets held two 50 caliber machine guns along with an additional two in the waist. The heavy bomber had a range of 2,800 miles and a ceiling of 32,000 feet. It had a wing span of 110 feet.

Harder to handle even with all of the improvements and upgrades of a heavier bomber load, the plane was unwieldy and vulnerable to battle damage. The fuselage was undependable and tended to break apart, making it difficult to ditch the aircraft or perform a successful belly landing, and was notorious for its tendency to catch on fire. She was nicknamed the "Flying Coffin" by some of the airmen. However, as a means to inspire his men, Stewart flew as command pilot in the new lead B-24.

Death and Duty

War was hell. And, training for war had had its heartbreaks.

As a B-17 instructor pilot back in Boise, Idaho, Stewart had lost a roommate, friends and several students while flying in the snow, ice and fog. Preparing bombing crews in the B-24 during summer in Sioux City had proved even more treacherous.

On August 26, 1943, one of the planes on a night training mission had crashed, killing all nine men on board.

On September 2, just before midnight, another plane plummeted to the ground killing all ten of the crew. It crashed so close to the base that horrified recruits had watched it burn. The next day, a third crash claimed eight more lives.

The men, already jumpy, felt jinxed.

That had been *before* they'd flown into battle with the German Luftwaffe. In the first 21 days of combat, they'd lost 60 men. Maintaining a low key and cheerful demeanor on the outside, inside he fought hand-to-hand combat with fear as they soared in the Nazi-infested skies.

"Fellas," Jimmy said, his gaze sweeping over his men as he briefed them, "the Germans have some kind of new rocket machine they've cooked up. They're going to use it to hit London and a lot of other cities over here in England. We've got to stop it before it goes that far.

"We're going to fly at 12,000 feet and hit those targets," he said, pointing at a map. A murmur of surprise rippled through the room. "Yeah, I said 12,000 feet. I know that 12,000 feet is pretty low for us heavies, but we have to *make sure* we hit those targets.

"I'm going to make this voluntary. That means anyone who doesn't want to go on a Christmas Eve mission doesn't have to go. No one will hold it against you. But I'm going. You can count on that.

"The target is Bonnieres, France. We'll be hitting the German's secret rocket emplacements there. Thirty-five aircraft from this group will go. Flak will be heavy, but you'll see the English coast most of the flight."

Living With Danger

Following the briefing, Captain Stewart walked to the hanger feeling the weight of command heavy on his lean frame. Bombing raids weren't the only danger the men encountered. England was a bombed-out shell of its former self and Nazi air raids attacked Tibenham on a regular basis.

Danger had become their constant companion.

Taxiing down the runway, Jimmy patted his pocket to make sure his father' letter was there. Back in the States, the ground echelon had left for England and the group's new Liberators had been parked on hard stands out in the field when he'd said goodbye to his parents. Grabbing Jimmy in a final hug, his father had pressed a sealed envelope into his hand. "Read this after you're airborne," he said, his voice thick with emotion. But, Jimmy had the letter opened by the time the plane had barely cleared the runway.

My dear Jim boy,

Soon after you read this letter you will be on your way to the worst sort of danger. I have had this in mind for a long time and I am very much concerned. But Jim, I am banking on the enclosed copy of the 91ˢᵗ Psalm. The thing that takes the place of fear and worry is the promise in these words. I feel sure that God will lead you through this mad experience... I can say no more. I continue only to pray. Goodbye my dear. God bless and keep you. I love you more than I can tell you.

Dad

Jimmy was never without that letter tucked in the pocket of his flight suit. According to plan, Stewart and his men spent Christmas Eve attacking the location of German secret weapon concentrations in France.

The fifth day of the blitz established two new records for the American Eighth Air Force, of which Stewart and his company were a part. They returned to Tibenham without losing a single plane.

Veering Off Course

Like all the enlistees, Stewart was given a small book with the Psalms, Proverbs and New Testament which could fit in a pocket. Each book included a letter from President Franklin D. Roosevelt. *"As Commander-in-Chief,*

I take pleasure in commending the reading of the Bible to all who serve in the armed forces of the United States. Throughout the centuries men of many faiths and diverse origins have found in the Sacred Book words of wisdom, counsel and inspiration. It is a fountain of strength and now, as always, an aid in attaining the highest aspiration of the human soul."

The battle of U.S. bombers against the German Luftwaffe was to the death. After numerous near-misses, Captain Stewart gained the reputation of a "lucky" pilot who always brought his crew home to safety, but his dependence on Psalm 91 kept Stewart going.

On January 7, 1944, Stewart, in command of the 445th Bomb Group returning from battle in a two group wing formation, discovered that the group he was following had made an error in navigation.

They were 30 degrees off course. They were flying into enemy territory.

Captain Stewart called the leader and pointed out the error in navigation. The leader insisted that Stewart was wrong.

Another formation left on course and Jimmy knew he could tack on behind them and ensure the safety of his crew. However, that would mean abandoning the leading group to their fate and making them easy prey.

With a sinking feeling in his heart, Stewart followed his leader. Twenty-eight miles south of Paris, the lead group was attacked by 60 Messerschmitt and Focke-Wulfs. Jimmy closed in for support and watched in horror as flames burst into the sky. The leader and some other B-24's had been shot down.

Outmatched, Jimmy's formation took on the German planes. The Focke-Wulfs didn't score a single kill. Once again, Jimmy brought his boys back alive.

Uncounted Flights

He and his men bombed the Nazi aircraft assembly in Leipzig, Regensurg, Gotha, Brunswick and Schweinfurt. Jimmy flew in the thick of it, bringing his crippled planes and grateful men back to base.

New orders from Washington commanded that each pilot would fly 30 missions instead of the original 25 before being reassigned. Stewart watched many men die while sweating out those last five missions.

"I can't just sit here and send these fellas to death," Stewart told his squadron adjunct with a determined glint in his eye. On his own orders, Stewart's missions into Nazi-occupied Europe went uncounted. Although the official number is recorded at 20, the true number will never be known.

Toward the end of the war, Stewart helped lead the attack against Berlin.

"Fear is an insidious and deadly thing," Colonel Stewart said after the war. "It can warp judgment, freeze reflexes and breed mistakes. Worse, it's contagious. I knew that my own fear, if not checked, could infect my crew members. And, I could feel it growing in me."

What he said about the psalm has often been quoted. Referring to Psalm 91, Colonel Stewart said, "What a promise for an airman! I placed in His Hands the squadron I would be leading. And, as the psalmist promised, I felt myself borne up."

Jimmy Stewart was one of only a few Americans to rise from private to colonel in four years as the war ended. He was the highest ranking actor in military history. During World War II, he earned the Air Medal, the Distinguished Flying Cross, the Croix de Guerre and seven battle stars. Active in the Air Force Reserve, in 1959 Stewart achieved the rank of Brigadier General and later flew combat duty in Vietnam.

Back in Hollywood after the war, Jimmy Stewart filmed one of the movies for which he is best known: *It's a Wonderful Life.*

Jimmy didn't just carry the letter during war time. He never quit carrying his father's letter with him for the rest of his life and died on July 7, 1997. Engraved on his tombstone is his favorite verse: Psalm 91:11.

For He shall give His angels charge over thee to keep thee in all thy ways.

Although angels did, indeed, keep Jimmy Stewart, his life could also be summed up in many aspects of Psalm 91 of the protection from terror, the arrows by day, the pestilence and the destruction. The promise found in Psalm 91: 14-16. "*... I will set him securely on high, because he has known My name ...I will rescue him and honor him... and give him a long life.*"

God delivered Jimmy Stewart from almost certain death and honored him with success, a good name and a long life.

For Jimmy Stewart, it was a wonderful life.

Because of a wonderful promise.

Used with Permission of Shirley Boone. Special Thanks to photographer John McGuire

Shirley Boone

My dear first grandson, Ryan Corbin, fell through a skylight of the roof of his apartment building over 13 years ago, on June 19th, 2001, when he was 24 years old. He nearly died! His mom, our daughter Lindy, was in Spain on vacation, so his roommates called to ask me to meet them at the Emergency Room of the UCLA Hospital. When the doctors came out to tell us Ryan's condition, they said his spleen was ruptured, his lungs collapsed, and they could not stop the bleeding. They looked at me very compassionately and said..."People in this condition don't usually make it." I heard their diagnosis with my ears, but, in my spirit, I heard Holy Spirit say to me a scripture in Psalms 118:17 "HE WILL LIVE AND NOT DIE, AND DECLARE THE

GLORY OF GOD." The scripture actually says "works of the Lord," but I heard "GLORY"...and total PEACE came. They were telling me my beloved grandson was not going to live through the night, but God was letting me know through His Word that Ryan was in His Hands, and there would be a different result. A MIRACLE!

Just days before his accident, Holy Spirit had told me to tell Ryan, who was totally committed to the Lord, to memorize as much of the 91st Psalm as he could. He said he would, but he found it hard to find the time, with work and other responsibilities...but he assured me it was his intent. A few days later, I received this urgent call to come to meet his roommates at the hospital. Now over 13 years later, his mom told me two days ago, that Peggy Joyce Ruth, at my request, had sent books and a CD with music and the 91st Psalm on it, and Lindy is going to play it over and over for him as he goes to sleep. He is able to memorize scripture, so we are waiting to watch the Lord bring forth His perfected work in Ryan. His Word is life and health to us. He is a champion and has been fighting the fight of faith.

When Ryan was a few months old, his parents asked if I could take care of Ryan while they went to Hawaii. I was going over to visit two of my daughters at YWAM, Youth With A Mission, on the island of Hawaii. They let me bring

Ryan with me. I had had some frightening experiences on planes, but after receiving the Baptism of the Holy Spirit, my fear of flying was gone...until I got on a small plane with this precious baby in my lap. Then the head of the roaring lion began to rise again. I prayed, "Please Lord, give me one of those scriptures about eagles flying." I could not think of one scripture. Suddenly, I heard in my spirit, "*Though a thousand fall on your left, and ten thousand on your right, no harm will come near you.*" Total peace, that passes all understanding, came all over me, and I KNEW we were okay. Psalms 91:7 was hidden in my heart, and brought the very thing I needed at that moment.

I told Ken Copeland about my experience a few days later, because he's a pilot. He said you know why the Lord didn't give you one of those eagle scriptures, don't you? I said, No! He said, "Well, you probably are not afraid of flying...you were afraid of falling." See how He went before me to prepare the way, and He knows what we have need of (better than I did), even before we ask?

That same peace is on me now...to know that Peggy Joyce Ruth has prepared the MEAT of the 91st Psalm in a form that will give strength to Ryan right where he is now, and it may complete the work that the Lord has begun. Please join us in praying for his SUDDENLY!

Michael Payne
Freelance Writer
(Five Times to Iraq)

In 1998, at the age of forty eight, I was constantly dogged with hopelessness and despair. I felt I was never going to smile again. I had spent thirty-three of those forty eight years drinking, drugging, gambling and committing multiple adulteries in vain attempts to grab temporary moments of what I thought would bring happiness. These things no longer brought any satisfaction or respite from the depression, thoughts of suicide and other symptoms attributed to PTSD that were now hounding me constantly. My second marriage was falling apart and my sons from my first marriage could no longer stand to be around me.

In the fall of 1998, a Christian from Guatemala, seeing the pain and distress in my face, said to me, "Brother Michael, I read Psalm 91 every day before I come to work!" He did not elaborate, but the SPIRIT of the LORD was at work and HE gave me ears to hear. I started reading Psalm 91 several times a day. Eventually, it brought, not only a smile to my face, but also a smile in my heart. I knew that the LORD was speaking directly to me and that HE was keeping all HIS promises in Psalm 91. There is not one part of Psalm 91 that I did not grab hold of and believe as a covering from the battles in my life. It not only saved my life, but the Psalm lead me to believe in GOD, and, one year later, I gave my life to JESUS.

I carry a handwritten copy of Psalm 91 in my wallet. It reminds me of the power of GOD'S WORD as I traveled through Iraq, Afghanistan and even right here in the U.S. I have been to Iraq four times as a freelance Christian radio reporter. I know the LORD saved my life on several specific occasions, and, many times, when I was not even aware. GOD is sovereign over every bullet and every piece of shrapnel that flies. HE gives me victory and peace and if we but stand in the shadow of the ALMIGHTY, HE will deliver us, without fail.

I am set free from alcohol, drugs, sexual sin, gambling, and worldly ways. I am not recovering from any of these; I am set free. I am a new creation in CHRIST JESUS! I owe it all to GOD and I owe it to the truth, the way and the life expressed in Psalm 91 and JESUS CHRIST.

Michael Payne
Winchester, Virginia
www.takeastandministries.org

Sergeant Harold Barclay
of Brownwood, Texas
as told by his daughter, Janie Boyd

Sergeant George Harold Barclay served in WWII in General Patton's 320th Infantry of the U.S. Army, Company E. Continuous fear eliminated any expectation of ever returning to his wife and baby daughter. The same fear kept his wife terrified when she would see a Western Union truck delivering letters of war casualties. Once a

Western Union messenger came to her door by mistake and she said that she froze with terror. Sometimes as many as six weeks would go by without a letter, during which time the News reported that half of Harold's company had been killed. The Battle of the Bulge saw his whole outfit cut off from the rest of the army.

Finally, however, a letter came from Harold saying that God had given him Psalm 91, and he now had absolute certainty that he would come home without even an injury. So certain was he of this promise in Psalm 91, that when the medics said they needed volunteers to go to the front lines to bring back the injured, Harold volunteered and made repeated trips under extreme enemy fire, saving many lives.

The citation for the Bronze Star Award that he received said "...for bravery", but Harold insisted that it wasn't bravery since he knew nothing would happen to him because of the covenant promise God had given to him in Psalm 91. When he came home without a scratch, it was obvious that *angels had indeed borne him up in their hands, allowing no evil to befall him.*

John G. Lake's Psalm 91 Testimony

I have often read accounts of the time when John G. Lake took fraught from the Bubonic Plague in his hand and placed it under a microscope where people watched in amazement as the germs literally died instantly on contact with his hand. I was puzzled for years, wondering what kind of anointing he had on his life to bring about this supernatural phenomenon.

Nothing could have pleased me more than when I learned Mr. Lake's secret—his wholehearted belief in the Psalm 91 protection that God has provided.

Mr. Lake made the statement that confirmed the secret to his supernatural protection—"For many years God kept me so that sickness and death could not touch me, **from the day that I saw in the ninety-first Psalm a man's privilege of entering into God, not only for healing, but *health* and having God and the life of God in every fiber of his being."[1]**

[1] *John G. Lake: The Complete Collection of His Life Teachings*, Albury Publishing, Tulsa, OK *p.340*. {Reprinted with kind permission]

Mary Johnson

Kidnapping Testimony

After just returning from a five day Red Brangus Cow sale where we also met our daughter to buy clothes for the soon-to-be-birthed, first grandchild, I had gotten an early start that morning to catch up on my chores. We live 12 miles in the country, so I was surprised to be interrupted by a young man in an old van—supposedly lost—asking for a drink of water. But, the pretense was over when he pulled a gun and told me to get in the car. My surprised scream was soon stifled, however, when he threatened my life if I did that again. I was thrown into the back of the van and a man wearing a nylon stocking on his head put athletic tape over my mouth and hands and covered my head with a black windbreaker. Black shag carpet covered the sides, floor and roof of the van and the windows were covered with black curtains.

I couldn't tell where they were taking me. I know that we crossed railroad tracks and ended up on a gravel road. I had never been so frightened in my life. All I could think about was that I was soon to be 50—soon to be a grandmother—and, I wasn't sure I would live to see either; but my greatest fear was being raped. Finally, however, I came to my senses and started claiming my spiritual covenant promise of protection. I suddenly realized—*I was a child of God—fear was of the devil—and I was trusting God that nothing would happen to me.*

By this time we had stopped and with a wool cap pulled down over my face, I was led over a barbed wire fence and across a pasture to an old abandoned ranch house where I was handcuffed to the bathroom lavatory and asked, "What would be the best way to get your husband to cooperate without alerting the police." Then I was warned that if he went to the police he would never see me again—alive! A phone call with all the usual kidnapping threats and instructions was planned, and then I was left to my dilemma.

Still quoting my promises, singing hymns of deliverance and thanking God, I was frantically working to get the pipes loose, but they wouldn't budge. God said in *Psalm 91:15: "In your day of trouble, call upon Me and I will answer."* I started praying, "Lord, I am calling on You! I can't do this, but You can. Show me a way to get loose." Then, for the first time I noticed a tiny pipe coming up the back of the sink. I don't have any idea how I was able to break through, but I know it was a miracle because later the FBI agent couldn't believe I was able to do what I did.

Feeling sure the kidnappers would make their call to Don and be back shortly, I was out the back door and over the fence in no time. I had no idea where I was, but I was confident God would get me where I needed to be. Twelve miles later I came to a house with every door locked except the front door. (I later found out that the lady never left her doors unlocked, except on this particular day.) After several calls the Sheriff was on his way to get me, but my husband had already left for Goldthwaite, Texas, with the ransom money.

The kidnappers skipped that first meeting but called at 12:30 that night with a new appointed place to meet in Austin, Texas. Obviously, they didn't know I had escaped. This time it was the Texas Rangers who met and took the first man into custody, and later, the second one was apprehended. I was called to Austin by the FBI to pick him out of a "line-up." All I asked was for the men in the line-up to wear a ball cap and say, "Would you get me a glass of water?" With that, I was able to successfully pick him out of the group and my job was over.

I thank God for His covenant of protection in Psalm 91. We do not have to be afraid of the *"terror of what man can do to us—it will not approach us when we run to God and dwell in His Shelter."*

[*The man who was convicted of this crime was no amateur criminal. According to police investigation he had a habitual crime problem since his youth and had previously been convicted and imprisoned for robbery, indecency and sexual assault. For this present offense he was sentenced to 99 years in prison. The sheriff told Mrs. Johnson that they had never had anyone in their local jail as malicious as this man. The FBI was shocked that Mrs. Johnson was able to escape and even more shocked that she had not been beaten, raped or murdered. One of the FBI made the comment, "We cannot believe we are sitting here today with you and that you are alive and well."]*

Remains of Elementary School

Tornado Protection Miracle
By Nikki McCurtain
Moore, Oklahoma

Smiling, I put the finishing touches on a gift. It was May 2013, the weekend before the last 4 days of school, which marked the end of my first year as a teacher at Plaza Towers Elementary School in Moore, Oklahoma. Call me sentimental, but I'd made gifts for all of my 26 students. I *loved* my job and knew I would never forget this class. I'd made each student a portfolio of their work, hoping they too would cherish the memories.

Humming, I walked across the room in our house in Norman, Oklahoma and froze. A picture freeze-framed in my mind's eye. I saw what looked like a war zone, and *I was walking through the debris*! I realized I was seeing a disaster, but what kind? Here in Oklahoma, we'd suffered a terrorist attack in 1995. Might there be another? It looked like *war.* Whatever it represented, I knew one thing for certain; God wanted me to pray.

Already alarmed, when the picture flashed in my view a second time, I knew for sure that some kind of disaster was about to happen. "Preston," I said to my husband, "we've got to pray!" I described the vision I'd seen and we began praying in the spirit, pleading for understanding.

The next day, Sunday, May 19, tornado sirens wailed in the afternoon as we took cover in a friend's storm shelter. Several tornadoes touched down north and east of us bringing death and destruction. I was tired by the time we got home that evening and turned on the news. It wasn't good. Meteorologists said that conditions were ripe for super cells. Most of the time those conditions don't fulfill their potential, but we've learned to keep an eye on the sky and stay abreast of the storm warnings.

On Monday, May 20, only 23 of my 26 students arrived for class. Some had been kept home because of the uncertain weather. Many of them had taken shelter the night before and that's all they wanted to talk about.

During journal time I said, "Okay, let's get out our journals and talk with our pencils."

The classroom fell quiet for a few minutes except for the scratching of pencils against paper. Taking care of some paperwork, I thought about the women's mentoring group I attended which was led by Rev. Barbara Stumprud and Julia Pickard. Back in February they suggested we read *Psalm 91: God's Umbrella of Protection* by Peggy Joyce Ruth. Although I was familiar with the Bible, I'd never studied that psalm of protection. I loved reading about the secret place of the Most High.

The 4th verse read, "*He will cover you with His pinions, and under His wings shall you trust and find refuge...*" The author explained that pinions are the strongest part of the wing. She compared this verse to a mother hen scooping her chicks under her wings for protection. For some reason I'd gotten stuck on this verse, reading it over and over. I couldn't seem to get past it.

The children finished journaling and around noon we had Café Time. I used my SmartBoard to project an image of a café on the wall, complete with coffee and biscotti. Students gathered around me and each one took a turn with the microphone, talking about things they'd written in their journal.

During recess, Preston showed up to take my car. "It's going to be bad," he said. *How bad?* I thought, looking up into dark, ominous clouds. I always prayed protection over my students and I'd anointed their desks with oil early in the school year. But, today was unusual; I'd spent every spare moment praying and listening for God.

Returning after recess, our 4th grade classes rotated and my class was much smaller in the afternoons. Parents picked up their students at a steady pace, and by 1:35 I only had 10 left. We all settled on the floor for reading time. The students were excited about our next chapter. I was reading *The Magician's Nephew*, one of the books in the *Chronicles of Narnia* series. The world of Narnia was in darkness, still in the process of being created. As Aslan sang, brilliant green grass sprang up out of the ground piercing the darkness with new life.

I paused and whispered, "This is such a powerful comparison between good and evil and how new life always grows out of darkness." Enrapt in the story, for a while we almost forgot the dark clouds gathering over our comfortable little world. Thunder bellowed outside our classroom shaking our walls as the hail began to fall.

There weren't many children left at school by 2:30 when the principal's words crackled over the loud speakers instructing everyone to take tornado precautions. We'd practiced enough over the school year that the kids knew the drill by heart.

They also knew this *wasn't* a drill.

The noise I heard approaching the school was louder than any train I'd ever heard. The ground vibrated like a train approaching the station. But, as it closed the distance to the school, it felt like an earthquake.

Scared and weeping, they formed a line in the hall. Outside tornado sirens shrilled as the children knelt and held a book over their heads just as we'd practiced. As we waited, calming the kids, more parents arrived…but it was too late to leave. They were trapped with us.

There were only about 40 people in our hall, 30 of them children. When the school is full, there are too many children to take shelter in the bathrooms. However, part of our disaster plan is that if we think that students might be in danger from breaking glass, we can move them into the restrooms. Our hall was dotted with large square lights which the other hallway didn't have. After a brief consultation with the other teachers, we decided to squeeze our group into the girl's bathroom.

"Scoot up! Scoot up!" I urged. As the tornado sirens screamed again, children crawled under the sinks and stacked like cordwood in the stalls. My back was facing the doorway and I was holding hands tightly with my co-teacher. We had to survive this together. Just then my cell phone rang, and I hadn't had reception before.

Preston had been watching the path of the tornado and was horrified to watch it tracking straight for the school. "I love you so much," he said, choking back tears.

"I love you too." As Preston and I said goodbye, fear and grief threatened to overwhelm me. *Would this goodbye be forever?* My cell phone went dead. Gasping, I jumped to my feet trying to get a breath. Swirling around, I stood facing the doorway to the hall—and watched, frozen in shock—as the tornado came near us. I took cover again hovering over a couple students. Massive brown, violent, swirling debris moved past us down the very hallway we'd just vacated. In my life I'd never felt a more demonic presence. The sense of evil was so overwhelming that a startling truth crossed my mind: *tornadoes are* not *an act of God!*

I didn't know if I had the spiritual strength for what we faced. "Lord, give me one verse to pray!" I cried.

The answer was delivered to me as I stayed in a prayer position. *"Psalm 91:4."* Personalizing the verse I prayed, *"He will cover us with His pinions and under His wings we will trust and find refuge!"* I prayed that verse over and over until someone pressed their hand to my back. Had another parent arrived and needed to squeeze inside? I turned to see who it was.

No one was there.

The fear was palpable. "These are my students!" I declared. "They *aren't* dying!"

The rumble of the approaching tornado was deafening, but I heard an assuring whisper. *Nikki, you're going to be okay.* Suddenly it felt like the earth shifted on its axis. Walls crashed, the roof lifted away. Pipes broke. Children screamed. Cement blocks flew through the air like twigs. Nothing prepared me for what came next.

The cacophony of sights and sounds indescribable, the building that had been our refuge from the world was reduced to nothing more than matchsticks of timber and desolation. My ears still roaring from the sound, I began pulling debris off of screaming children. Many of them had head wounds, cuts, scrapes, and they were all terrified. "It's okay!" I said to screaming children as we pulled them out of the rubble. "You're alive!" Everyone was in shock. The kids were cold and shivering, bloody and caked with mud and debris, but they were all alive.

My brave co-teacher Mrs. Martinez helped our student, Makaila, out of the rubble. With a tear-stained face Makaila said, "I knew I was going to be okay because I asked God to put us in protective bubbles."

As I stepped out onto the debris to view the scene, my breath hitched. It looked like a bulldozer had razed the school. *It was the exact image that had flashed before my eyes twice over the weekend.* I later found out that children in the other hallway were ushered into heaven and into the Lord's glorious light on that day.

I often think back to May 20, 2013. *How did I stand so close to an EF-5 tornado, watching it pass, and not get sucked into the vortex?* It's as though we were in the secret place of the Most High, a place so supernatural that a child might describe it as a protective bubble.

I still recall the pressure on my back. And, I remember how the Lord directed me to pray Psalm 91:4, *He will cover you with His pinions..."* I don't believe that what I felt was a hand. It was the Lord covering us, scooping us *under His wing* for protection.

Don Beason

US Navy WWII veteran

Our good friend, Don Beason, sent me this documentation on the tornadoes which devastated Grand Island, Nebraska and then told his unique story of what took place in the midst of that horrible natural disaster. Mark Getzfred, an independent staff writer for the newspaper, wrote the following:

"Three, possibly four, tornadoes grouped together and slashed their way down Bismark Rd and S. Locust St. Roger Wakimoto, an assistant for Dr. Fujital of Chicago

University, said his preliminary research shows the movement of the tornadoes during the June 3 storm was extremely erratic. According to Wakimoto it was a very unusual tornado case, seeming to have changed directions moving west down Bismark Rd from Knesters Lake and then making a sharp left turn onto South Locust Street. Fujital said the smaller tornadoes began spinning around the larger one and as they began picking up debris, they locked together forming one large tornado. Don Davis, chief meteorologist with the National Weather Service in Grand Rapids said there was a counterclockwise movement of the front, the main tornado came in the second movement and the smaller tornadoes followed behind, creating one of the worst of its kind ever recorded. In all, there were at least seven tornadoes all going in different directions, but four of them came together to make a large one that did most of the damage."

Interestingly, the tornado at Grand Island was headed directly for Mr. Beason's office and the first of the two erratic, unexplainable turns the tornado made was only a few yards before it reached him. It ruined the office directly across the street, but not even a window was cracked in his office. The second of the two radical changes of direction was just before it would have swept through Mr. Beason's farm. The farms next to his were all destroyed. The city map showing the tornado's path confirmed its going straight to his office, then turning in front of his doorstep and going straight for his farm, then once again, turning just short of his property line. The chart dramatically showed the two major surprise changes of direction were directly related to his real estate. There was no explanation in the natural for the two sudden turns of the tornado—but no one could convince Mr. Beason it was not the direct result of God's Psalm 91 protection he had been claiming— *"I will not be afraid of the destruction (natural disasters) that lay waste at noon."*

***

A few years later the TV station reported a mile-wide tornado heading once again toward Grand Island. Mr. Beason said, "I went outside and rebuked it and commanded it to turn away and disappear. A minute or two later when I went back into the house, the TV announcer said the tornado had lifted out of sight." Beason said, *"This was just more of God's Psalm 91 protection!"*

Stella Marshall

*I could hardly believe what my eyes were seeing and my ears
hearing as I sat in Ms Stella Marshall's room and listened to her
life story. Watching her have no need for glasses or a hearing
aid, hearing her answer questions with the sharp mind of a
twenty year old, and noticing that she didn't have to take her
teeth out at night, I was in awe when Stella told me all about
her* **ninety fifth** *birthday party she had enjoyed the day before. (I
would have guessed her to be not a day over seventy years old.)
From the moment I heard some of her fellow church members
refer to her as the "Psalm 91 Lady" I was determined to get an
interview with this beautiful woman. Truly, she is the epitome
of someone who has been* **"satisfied with a long life"** *and* **"kept
safe"** *by the power of Psalm 91.*

Stella Marshall's maternal grandfather came as a young boy by ship to Virginia from Africa where his own people had sold him and his mother and father as slaves. Stella's mother was one of his eighteen children. Stella's father, on the other hand, had a much different background. His mother was Irish and it was his sister who later took Stella and her younger brother and sister to rear when their dad died at age twenty-eight after receiving a head injury at the Ennis railroad yard where he worked. Stella, who picked cotton most of her young life, married at sixteen *for the sole purpose of never having to pick cotton again,* but her dreams of how married life would be did not turn out as she had planned. She had envisioned having a long table with benches on each side where the family would gather for meals—six boys on one side facing the six girls across from them, and she and her husband sitting at each end of the table. Her idea of how a marriage should be was shattered when it ended in divorce and she was left with three children to rear alone. She had been brought up in a Baptist home, but there was no real relationship with the Lord so worldliness quickly took hold of her life. Finally, in desperation, at age fifty-four, Stella stood by the fence in her front yard and said, "God, You see these cigarettes in my hand? When I smoke these, I'm not going to smoke ever again. I'm not going to take another drink and I'm not going to be with another man as long as I live." She kept that promise, but for the next five years she could not find satisfaction for the longing and the hungering in her heart for a deeper walk with God. In August, 1971, five years after she had given up her flesh life, she asked Jesus in her heart and to be Lord of her life. She was prayed over to receive the Baptism of the Holy Spirit and everything in her life changed. She said that each night she would go to sleep and see Jesus standing over her with His hands outstretched. Before receiving the Baptism of the Holy Spirit she had read her Bible with very little understanding, but after being prayed for, Stella said that she was getting something new every time she opened her Bible. Every Full Gospel meeting found Stella on the front row. She couldn't get enough of the Lord.

When I asked Stella why her friends called her the *Psalm 91 Lady*, she said, "When I found Psalm 91 I have prayed it over myself and over my family every single day since, and I tell everyone I see about God's wonderful protection." I was curious how she happened to find it and she told me an interesting story. She was asked to go to Dallas to keep the grandbaby of the fifth richest man in Texas. The servant's quarters where she lived was secluded back behind the big mansion. Not being accustomed to staying alone, she began to think about the real possibility of someone breaking into a rich man's property. She got very fearful because she knew that no one would be able to see or hear her if she needed help—so she began crying out to God to take away all her fears. Faithful to His promises, God supernaturally lead her to Psalm 91 and she has been saying it everyday since. Those angels that God placed in charge of her and the confidence that began to build with the knowledge that God had answered her cry, developed such faith in God's Psalm 91 covenant of protection that she has been kept from harm from that day forth and satisfied with a long life. Stella recalled the time when a flu virus slipped in on her and she began to stand for her healing. When the symptoms didn't leave right away, she said, *"Lord, You said if we asked anything, You would do it. I've been expecting my healing. If I haven't heard from You by tomorrow, I am going to the doctor, but my trust is in You."* Then, she turned over and went to sleep. About 6:30 a.m. Stella said that something woke her up, saying, "You are healed." She said that there was not a place on her that wasn't well. Where she had been struggling to breathe, she could now breathe with ease.

Stella, who has practically raised many of her grandchildren and great-grandchildren, never misses a night praying Psalm 91 over every one of them.

Because of her belief in God and the many blessings He has poured out on her life, Stella wanted to find some way to do something to help others; therefore, in her early 60's Stella started a routine that lasted over 20 years. She would buy stalks of bananas with her own money and distribute them to the residents of nursing homes. She was such a regular visitor that the director of one of the homes scheduled "The Banana Lady" as an activity all by herself. No matter what the weather, Stella never missed her Thursday afternoon appointment. She never worried if she would have money for her bananas. When Thursday came, the money was always there. For over twelve years Stella also volunteered at the Casa de Amigos' Health Clinic getting files and signing people in. And, all of that is in addition to helping raise her eight grandchildren and thirteen great-grandchildren.

I have often said that just having a lot of birthdays is not always a blessing. It takes a *satisfied* life to make long life good. You don't have to ask Stella if she is satisfied with her life. Just as obvious as her dissatisfaction with life was before age fifty-four, her satisfaction since then has been just as obvious.

Copy and enlarge his **Psalm 91 prayer** to pray over yourself and your loved ones, inserting his or her name in the blanks.

_____ dwells in the shelter of the Most High and (he/she) will abide in the shadow of the Almighty. _____ says to the LORD, "My refuge and my fortress, My God, in whom I trust!" For it is He who delivers _____from the snare of the trapper and from the deadly pestilence. The Lord will cover _____ with His pinions, and under His wings _____ may seek refuge; His faithfulness is a shield and bulwark. _____ will not be afraid of the terror by night, or of the arrow that flies by day; of the pestilence that stalks in darkness, or of the destruction that lays waste at noon. A thousand may fall at _____'s side and ten thousand at his or her right hand, *but* it shall not approach _____. _____will only look on with your eyes and see the recompense of the wicked. For _____has made the LORD, his/her refuge, e*ven* the Most High, _____'s dwelling place. No evil will befall _____, Nor will any plague come near_____'s tent. For He will give His angels charge concerning _____, to guard _____ in all his/her ways. They will bear _____ up in their hands, that _____does not strike his/her foot against a stone. _____ will tread upon the lion and cobra, the young lion and the serpent _____ will trample down.

"Because _____ has loved Me, [God said] therefore I will deliver him/her; I will set _____ *securely* on high, because he/she has known My name. "_____ will call upon Me, and I will answer him/her; I will be with _____ in trouble; I will rescue _____ and honor him/her. "With a long life I will satisfy _____ and let _____ see My salvation."

183

Peggy Joyce Ruth has a unique way of showing that victorious living depends upon our unwavering trust in God. She demonstrates with scores of personal experiences just how faithful God really is and details how you can develop that kind of trust which will not disappoint.

This is the true story of someone who prayed "God, Never let my Life be Boring!" You'll be amazed at how God answered that prayer. There is non-stop action with twists and turns as Bibles are smuggled past armed guards into a Communist land. (by Angelia Schum, Peggy Joyce's daughter)

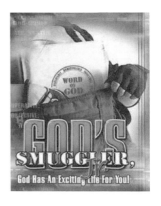

The personal testimony of Peggy Joyce Ruth. Her struggle through eight tormenting years of emotional illness, electrical shock treatments, prescription drugs and hopelessness—culminated in absolute victory made possible only by God's supernatural delivering power. Also gives step-by-step instructions on how to appropriate deliverance and advice.

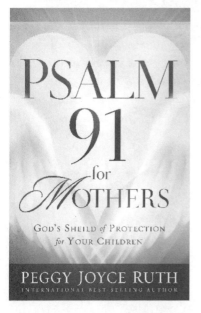